Privacy and Data Protection Law in China

Privacy and Data Protection Law in China

Chengxin Peng

Guosong Shao

This book was originally published as a monograph in the International Encyclopaedia of Laws/Privacy and Technology Law.

Founding Editor: Roger Blanpain
General Editor: Frank Hendrickx
Volume Editors: Jos Dumortier, Pieter Gryffroy, Ruben Roex & Yung Shin Van Der Sype

Wolters Kluwer

Published by:
Kluwer Law International B.V.
PO Box 316
2400 AH Alphen aan den Rijn
The Netherlands
E-mail: lrs-sales@wolterskluwer.com
Website: www.wolterskluwer.com/en/solutions/kluwerlawinternational

Sold and distributed by:
Wolters Kluwer Legal & Regulatory U.S.
920 Links Avenue
Landisville, PA 17538
United States of America
E-mail: customer.service@wolterskluwer.com

DISCLAIMER: The material in this volume is in the nature of general comment only. It is not offered as advice on any particular matter and should not be taken as such. The editor and the contributing authors expressly disclaim all liability to any person with regard to anything done or omitted to be done, and with respect to the consequences of anything done or omitted to be done wholly or partly in reliance upon the whole or any part of the contents of this volume. No reader should act or refrain from acting on the basis of any matter contained in this volume without first obtaining professional advice regarding the particular facts and circumstances at issue. Any and all opinions expressed herein are those of the particular author and are not necessarily those of the editor or publisher of this volume.

ISBN 978-94-035-0118-5

e-Book: ISBN 978-94-035-0128-4
web-PDF: ISBN 978-94-035-0138-3

The Authors

Chengxin Peng (born in June 1973) is a Dean and Distinguished Professor of Koguan Law School of Shanghai Jiao Tong University, China. He is also a Standing Member of the Civil Law Division of the China Law Society and the Vice President of the Civil Law Division of the Shanghai Law Society. He has been a visiting scholar or visiting professor at the Law Department of Oxford University, the Law Department of the London School of Economics and Political Science, Harvard Law School, Berkeley Law School, the "Academia Sinica" Institute of Law in Taiwan, and the Graduate School of Law of Hokkaido University. His research interests include principles of civil law, property law, data law, personal information protection, etc. He has published more than 100 articles in such journals as *Zhongguo Faxue (China Legal Science) and Faxue Yanjiu (Chinese Journal of Law)*. He has also authored or edited more than fifteen books, some of which have won several research awards at the national or provincial level.

Guosong Shao (born in July 1976) is the Director of the Center for Media and Public Affairs at Shanghai Jiao Tong University, China. He holds a PhD in mass communication from the University of Alabama, United States. His research interests include media law, Internet law, and Internet governance. He has published more than sixty articles in such journals as *Internet Research, Communication Research, Telematics & Informatics, and Computer Law & Security Review*. He is the single author of two books of *Internet Law in China (in English) and Introduction to Digital Media Law (in Chinese)*.

The Authors

Table of Contents

Funding Information

This work was supported by the National Social Science Fund of China (Award Number: 23AFX014 & 19ZDA328) and the Shanghai Education Committee Research Fund (Award Number: 2019-01-07-00-02-E00010).

Funding Information

Background

§1. Information Infrastructure in China

1. Information infrastructure includes the network communication layer, the storage and computing layer, and the integrated application layer. The network communication layer primarily consists of 4G and 5G networks, fiber optic broadband, IPv6, and satellite Internet. The storage and computing layer refers to data centers, cloud computing, and artificial intelligence. The integrated application layer involves the digitization of generic software and hardware infrastructure and traditional infrastructure, with a focus on industrial internet, Internet of Things (IoT), basic software, intelligent transportation infrastructure, and smart energy infrastructure. From 2012 to 2021, the number of Internet users in China increased from 564 million to 1.032 billion, and the Internet penetration rate rose from 42.1% to 73%. China possesses the world's largest 5G network and fiber optic broadband network, with the number of 5G base stations reaching 1.854 million and more than 455 million 5G mobile phone users. It is predicted that by 2025, 5G will directly create over 3 million jobs.

2. Both information infrastructure and traditional infrastructure possess general properties, such as being foundational, public, and exhibiting externalities, but they differ significantly in terms of service objects, technical-economic characteristics, application scenarios, and investment models. In terms of service objects, traditional infrastructure serves industrial society, providing tangible resources for production, supporting the circulation and application of atoms and energy. In contrast, digital infrastructure serves a digital society, providing intangible data and information resources, supporting the circulation and application of bits and computing power. In terms of technical-economic characteristics, traditional infrastructure focuses on heavy assets or asset-intensive industries, with limited room for technological advancement. The marginal output benefits show a downward trend. However, digital infrastructure emphasizes light assets, rapid technology iteration, a relatively short value lifespan, fierce competition, strong replaceability, tremendous long-term supply function, and high marginal output benefits. In terms of application scenarios, traditional infrastructure supports urbanization and industrial development, traditional industries such as agriculture, commerce, logistics, and manufacturing, and its application scenarios have been fully exploited. Meanwhile, digital infrastructure emphasizes interconnectivity among people, between people and objects, and between objects, supporting the transformation and development of digitization, networking, and intelligence, new industries, new formats and new models, industrial integration development, and new emerging consumer demand scenarios. In terms of investment models, traditional infrastructure is predominantly government-led investment, while digital infrastructure advocates primarily enterprise-led investment models.

3. In response to the impact of the COVID-19 pandemic, China has proposed to accelerate the construction of digital infrastructure. First, it aims to strengthen data management capabilities and stimulate the potential of data sources. This includes improving the policy and legal system for data governance, promoting the sharing and openness of government data, exploring innovative data management, and strengthening data security control and protection. This critical measure actually connects with the "Data Security Law." Second, it aims to innovate investment and construction models and give full play to the role of the market. On the one hand, it insists on market-oriented investment, supports multiple entities to participate in construction, and encourages financial institutions to innovate products and services. On the other hand, the government establishes rules for the digital infrastructure industry, and guides and supports orderly market operation through classified management. Third, it aims to deepen open cooperation and establish a good open source ecological environment. It encourages large enterprises to improve their contributions to the construction of the open source ecosystem, actively expands multilevel open source cooperation between Chinese companies and international organizations, and improves the open source risk emergency response system. Lastly, it aims to strengthen independent innovation and assessment certification to ensure supply security. On the one hand, it strengthens the independent research and development of key core technology products, actively cultivates autonomous ecosystems such as operating systems and artificial intelligence, and deeply promotes the construction of industrial Internet networks, platforms, and security systems. On the other hand, it accelerates the formulation of safety-related standards for the construction of digital infrastructure, standardizes the safety certification requirements of the entire industry chain, including design, development, production, application, services, etc., and accelerates safety certification assessments, such as the "Data Export Security Evaluation Measures" issued by China's Cyberspace Administration in July 2022.

4. The overall layout goals of China's digital infrastructure are as follows. First, in the short term, new infrastructure investment will directly play a role in boosting the economy, clarifying the expectations of stable growth and employment, and releasing potential economic vitality. The upstream and downstream of the relevant industrial chain will be directly stimulated by demand, offsetting the pressure of economic downturn. Second, in the long run, China's forward-looking layout of new infrastructure construction in response to the future global digital economy trend is expected to improve the economic development structure in the long term and nurture new economic development momentum. Third, it will stimulate the research and development application of new materials, new devices, new processes, and new technologies, providing necessary support for the development of new technologies, and the formation and large-scale commercialization of new industries, new models, and new forms. Fourth, it will promote integrated management based on digital platforms by various departments such as municipal administration, transportation, safety, environment, and informatization for new infrastructure, which will bring changes to the management model of government public infrastructure.

§2. E-COMMERCE IN CHINA

5. In the past decade or so, the rapid development of e-commerce has provided a new space for mass entrepreneurship and innovation, becoming the driving force for the development of the new economy. Therefore, promoting the development of e-commerce has become the basic policy direction of China's economic development. In 2015, the State Council issued the "Opinions on Vigorously Developing E-commerce and Accelerating the Cultivation of New Economic Dynamics." Since then, the State Council Office and relevant departments have issued a series of documents to promote the development of e-commerce. The "E-commerce Law" enacted in 2018 emphasizes the promotion of development as its fundamental legislative goal and transforms the above-mentioned policy guidelines into law. The scope of e-commerce under this law has been clearly defined to include not only traditional platform shopping but also shopping in online social circles and through live streaming. It therefore brings micro-merchants, proxy shoppers, and live-streaming sellers under its regulatory umbrella. While the "E-commerce Law" predominantly presides over e-commerce transactions within China, it does not extend its jurisdiction to cross-border e-commerce activities. As these activities are fundamentally considered import and export trade, they fall under the regulation of various other laws such as the "Customs Law of the People's Republic of China," "The Border Health Quarantine Law of the People's Republic of China," and "The Goods Import and Export Management Regulations of the People's Republic of China," among others.

6. Based on relevant laws, e-commerce refers to commercial activities carried out using information networks (including the Internet, mobile Internet, etc.). Commercial activities refer to business operations conducted with profit-making intentions, which include selling goods and providing services. The transfer of personal secondhand goods between individuals does not fall under business operations. Issues that exist in traditional offline transactions, such as infringement of consumer rights, infringement of intellectual property rights, unfair competition, and illegal transactions, also frequently appear in e-commerce transactions. The scope, magnitude, and potential harm of these problems are amplified in the realm of e-commerce due to its characteristics, such as broad geographical coverage, boundless virtual space, and rapid information exchange. Simultaneously, e-commerce has seen the emergence of novel issues that breach principles of honesty in business conduct, fair trade, and equitable competition, including phenomena like price discrimination through big data, inflated sales through fake orders, and over-collection and misuse of user data. It is only by enforcing regulations on e-commerce practices, assuring ethical business conduct, legality, and fair competition, can we safeguard the lawful rights of all stakeholders, preserve an orderly marketplace, and realize the objective of fostering continuous development.

7. China encourages and promotes the development of new types of e-commerce and innovation in business models. The development of e-commerce not only depends on the innovation of business models but also on the research, development, and application of technology. Therefore, in the fields of artificial intelligence, big data, cloud computing, and others, market entities of e-commerce actively develop and promote new technologies. They primarily use businesses as the main body, uniting with universities and scientific research institutions to establish key technical standards for e-commerce. Moreover, because e-commerce activities have characteristics of cyberspace, it is even more necessary to emphasize the construction of an Internet-based credit system. This involves perfecting the sharing mechanism of credit information resources among related departments, constructing an online credit information service platform, and achieving dynamic collection, processing, and exchange of credit data.

8. The "E-Commerce Law" is the basic and comprehensive law for e-commerce activities. E-commerce is essentially a transactional activity, and the most fundamental purpose of legal adjustment of private relationships is to protect the rights and interests of the parties involved. The e-commerce ecosystem is extremely complicated and multifaceted, with participants that include not only the contractual parties directly involved in transactions, such as operators and consumers, but also intellectual property rights holders, platform operators, and all types of entities providing other online services for e-commerce, such as payment, logistics, credit rating, and promotion of goods and services. In the specific provisions of the "E-Commerce Law" aimed at protecting rights and interests, consumer protection occupies a very important position. For example, many consumers have clearly purchased products of poor quality, but their authentic reviews have "disappeared" from the comment section. As a legal response, Article 39 of the "E-Commerce Law" explicitly prohibits the removal of reviews. Also, Article 18 of the "E-Commerce Law" also requires e-commerce platforms to introduce an option that allows users to turn off "personalized recommendations" to limit the practice of price discrimination based on big data.

§3. E-Government in China

9. Improving the level of digital government construction is the goal of China's e-government development. Article 37 of the "Data Security Law" stipulates that "the state vigorously promotes the construction of e-government, improves the scientificity, accuracy, and timeliness of government data, and enhances the ability to use data to serve the economic and social development." This is the first time that the development and utilization of government data have been explicitly supported and encouraged in law. With the widespread application of emerging technologies such as the Internet, big data, blockchain, and artificial intelligence, China is gradually forming smart governance models in areas like smart government, smart justice, smart procuratorial work, and smart security. In other words, the widespread application of digital technology in government management services is promoting the reconstruction of government governance processes and model optimization, constantly improving decision-making scientificity and service efficiency.

10. China vigorously promotes the construction of e-government mainly from the following three aspects. The first is to strengthen the open sharing of public data. Public data, also known as government data, refers to the data produced or obtained by the government in the process of performing its duties. Article 41 of the "Data Security Law" stipulates that "state organs should follow the principles of fairness, impartiality, and convenience, and promptly and accurately publicize government data as stipulated. Exceptions are those that shall not to be disclosed according to law." The current problem in China is insufficient data openness. Therefore, openness should be the principle and non-disclosure the exception, so as to maximize the opening of government data. However, the development and utilization of this type of data are continuously being promoted, and China is gradually building a nationwide integrated data sharing and exchange platform. Article 42 of the "Data Security Law" states that "the state formulates a government data opening catalogue, constructs a unified, standardized, interconnected, safe and controllable government data opening platform, and promotes the open use of government data." That is, the state establishes a data resource catalog and responsibility list system, enhances the functions of the national data sharing and exchange platform, and strengthens the sharing and utilization of basic information resources such as national population, legal persons, spatial geography, etc. In particular, it is necessary to strengthen the safe and orderly opening of basic public data, explore the inclusion of public data services into the public service system, construct a unified platform for opening national public data, and prioritize the opening of high-value data sets such as those of business registration, health, transportation, meteorology to the public.

11. The second is to promote the joint construction of government informatization. China is increasing its overall efforts in the construction of government informatization; improving the list of government informatization projects; deepening the integration of government information systems; and planning the construction of major information systems such as rule of law, market supervision, public safety, and ecological environment, to enhance cross-departmental governance capabilities. Specifically, it is improving the national e-government network, intensively building a government cloud platform and data center system, and promoting the cloud migration of government information systems. It is also strengthening the rapid iteration of government informatization construction, enhancing the rapid deployment capabilities and elastic expansion capabilities of government information systems. Of course, when the government collects and uses data in performing its statutory duties, it should also have clear legal regulations and follow basic principles. Article 38 of the "Data Security Law" requires state organs to "keep confidential the personal affairs, personal information, trade secrets, confidential business information and other data known in the performance of their duties according to law, and they shall not disclose or illegally provide them to others." This provision emphasizes the data confidentiality obligation of state organs, strengthens the institutional constraints on the collection and use of data by state organs, and is conducive to promoting state organs to continuously improve their data security capabilities.

12. The third is to enhance the efficiency of digital government services, actively promoting the digitization and intelligentization of government operations, business processes, and service models. For example, the "Regulations on Government Information Disclosure" have strict time limits for the processing of public information requests, requiring relevant government departments to respond promptly to the public's demand for information disclosure. Also, the implementation of "Internet+ Government Services" is advancing the capabilities of a fully integrated online service platform that supports all related government processes. For instance, the National Medical Insurance Service Platform website, established in China in 2020, officially launched the nationwide autonomous query service for cross-provincial medical treatment, providing a variety of practical and convenient online services such as insurance payment, information query, benefits application, and business handling. The China Higher Education Student Information website has launched more than twenty information systems, including the academic query system, online verification system, online registration and admission check system for postgraduate students, postgraduate enrollment adjustment service system, and the online office system for academic certification, thus achieving one-stop queries for national higher education information. In addition, China is accelerating the construction of digital technology-assisted government decision-making mechanisms, particularly emphasizing the use of digital technology in responding to sudden public events such as public health, natural disasters, accident disasters, and social security, thereby comprehensively enhancing early warning and emergency response capabilities.

§4. Social Media in China

13. Social media refers to internet-based platforms and applications that allow users to create and share content and participate in social networking. These platforms facilitate communication and interaction between users, enabling them to post messages and comments, share links, and upload images or videos. In China, the development of social media has roughly gone through the following stages. Before 2009, the landscape of social networks was dominated by platforms primarily designed for personal computers. However, from 2010 to 2014, a transition towards mobile-centric social networks occurred. These mobile social media platforms retained the core functionalities of traditional social media while introducing new features such as enhanced mobility, convenience, and smart capabilities. This evolution allowed users to access and engage with these applications seamlessly, regardless of time or location. From 2015 to 2018, there was a shift towards the creation of multimedia platforms that were designed around user interests. Beginning in 2019, immersive communities have sprung up, leveraging technologies such as 5G, artificial intelligence, and virtual reality. Currently, social media platforms have garnered a vast and diverse user base spanning all age groups. The most popular social media networks are WeChat, Weibo, and Douyin, each boasting user counts in the hundreds of millions.

14. However, the development of social platforms brings about various problems. First, under mixed operation, there are multiple entities involved in the operational chain, including the platform, streamers, brands, sellers, and consumers, which may give rise to multiple legal relationships. Moreover, complex platforms require sector-specific regulation, which can easily lead to regulatory overlaps or regulatory gaps. Second, platforms have dual identities as market entities and regulatory entities, which sometimes results in lax regulations on the qualifications of platform operators and the supervision of product information. Third, there are shortcomings in the protection of personal information, including illegal collection and excessive collection. Lastly, based on the industry model and dominant position of "one-to-many" on the platform, there are still numerous cases where platforms exempt themselves from liability through unilateral changes in the terms and conditions or stipulate "agreement upon use," thereby infringing upon consumer rights. Therefore, strengthening the governance of social platforms has become an important aspect of building a sound digital ecosystem. Specific measures include: (1) strengthening the protection of intellectual property rights for new products and new business methods, particularly in areas such as online games, videos, and education, to guide the standardized and orderly development of new business lines; (2) regulating acts of infringement on personal rights by social media platforms in accordance with the law. Internet platforms should balance the protection of personal information and the reasonable use of data, regulate acts of arbitrary collection, illegal acquisition, and excessive use of personal information; and (3) actively promote collaborative governance of cyberspace. Particularly, Internet platforms should fulfill their regulatory obligations commensurate with their business interests in a prudent manner.

§5. Digital Governance in China

15. China's digital governance exhibits the following characteristics. First, it emphasizes the idea of empowering technology and pursuing a balance of rights and interests. Rights are generally regarded as the legal expression of interests for individuals, and the more benefits created by human beings, the richer the content of rights becomes. In contrast to agrarian and industrial societies, the benefits of digital society are largely created through the use of personal information, and the allocation of property rights over personal information is primarily achieved through technological empowerment. This opens up a perspective of technological empowerment that differs from the views of monarchical power and natural human rights. For example, social media platforms such as WeChat and Weibo have replaced traditional social interactions, and electronic payment methods like WeChat Pay and Alipay have gradually replaced traditional payment models. These developments have led to the self-empowerment of the platforms and have "pressured" the government to recognize and make institutional changes. Furthermore, in the context of technological empowerment, there is a trend towards "powerization of technology" and "technologization of power." "Powerization of technology" refers to enterprises, mainly platform-based, creating their own rules based on their operational models, capital, and technological advantages. While the government imposes responsibilities on platforms through laws like the "Personal Information Protection Law," it also exercises "regulatory power" over platforms, such as the authority to impose restrictions, issue warnings, impose fines, and take down content, through technological regulations. In the context of China's e-government development, "technologization of power" represents the utilization of internet technology, digital technology, and artificial intelligence to empower the government in achieving objectives such as smart governance, a technologically advanced judiciary, and efficient law enforcement.

16. The governance of China's data society emphasizes the transformation towards the rule of law. The fifth part of the "14th Five-Year Plan for National Economic and Social Development of the People's Republic of China and Outline of Long-Range Objectives Through the Year 2035," published in 2021, clearly defines the strategic objective of "accelerating digital development and building a digital China." The operation of rule of law in the digital society should not only adhere to the core concept of modern rule of law but also reflect the governance logic of the digital society, emphasizing good governance. First, China has established a comprehensive legal framework for digital governance, which is embodied in new data-related legislation such as the "Civil Code," "Cybersecurity Law," "Data Security Law," and "Personal Information Protection Law." These laws all try to strike a balance between data use and personal information protection. Second, Chinese legislation has advocated the concept of digital justice, responding to issues such as the digital divide, algorithmic black boxes, algorithmic discrimination, and user profiling. For example, Article 24 of the "Personal Information Protection Law" regulates algorithmic automated decision-making, and Article 26 regulates the use of image collection and personal identity recognition devices in public places. Third, China's digital governance promotes the concept of digital human rights, using a series of legislation such as personal information processing rules to prevent and limit the overreach and misuse of technology by government authorities and digital platforms. Fourth, large Chinese Internet companies and platforms have proposed concepts such as "technology for good" and "friendly AI." This signifies a shared belief that technological advancements should primarily serve the "people," enhance the quality of human life and empower individuals to be the controllers instead of being the "prisoners" in an information-driven society. Fifth, China is laying the groundwork for a digital rules system with an aim to foster an open, robust, and secure digital ecosystem. This involves the development and refinement of market rules for data components, the creation of a standardized and well-regulated policy environment, an emphasis on bolstering cybersecurity, and an initiative towards building a shared future in cyberspace. The notion of a "shared future" encourages international dialogue and collaboration in cyberspace and the formulation of global digital rules, drawing on the United Nations as the primary conduit and the UN Charter as the fundamental principle. China is advocating a global internet governance system that is multilateral, democratic, and transparent, along with a fair and equitable framework for network infrastructure and resource management. It is actively contributing to the development of international regulations and standards for digital technology in areas such as data security, digital currencies, and digital taxation. Furthermore, China is propelling the development of a global cybersecurity cooperation mechanism and forging an international cooperation system for data protection, cybersecurity incident management, and cybercrime prevention. In addition, China offers digital assistance such as technology, equipment, and services to less developed countries, enabling all countries to share the benefits of the digital age.

Part I. Privacy Protection Legislation

§1. Privacy Protection in the Constitution

17. The Chinese Constitution does not explicitly stipulate the right to privacy. The constitutional basis for privacy rights is "personal freedom and dignity." Unlike the provisions of the EU's personal data protection framework, the right to privacy in China is not a basic right explicitly stipulated at the constitutional level. It is also different from the privacy rights system developed from the Fourth Amendment to the U.S. Constitution; China's right to privacy has not been constructed as an autonomous privacy right derived from the constitutional.

18. Although the term "privacy right" is not explicitly specified in the Chinese Constitution, the Constitution contains the value pursuit of privacy protection. It is mainly reflected in Article 33, which requires the state to "respect and protect human rights," Article 37, which explicitly states that "the personal freedom of citizens shall not be violated," Article 38, which indicates that the "personal dignity of citizens shall not be violated," and Articles 39 and 40, which respectively protect "the inviolability of the home" and "freedom and confidentiality of correspondence" for citizens.

19. The privacy rights and interests stipulated in the Civil Code are essentially in line with the interests of "personal freedom and dignity" enshrined in the Constitution. In abstract terms, the constitutional protection of general personality rights is concretized as general personality rights in the Civil Code. There are two pathways of connection between the two: First, understanding the legal nature of the Chinese Constitution, namely, that the Chinese Constitution serves as the fundamental law that protects the interests of citizens, such as privacy and personal dignity, against infringements by the state in activities involving personal information handling. Second, private rights always fall within the consideration of the constitution-makers, meaning that the state actively provides protection to ensure that individual dignity is not infringed upon by third parties.[1]

20. The clauses regarding "human rights" and "personal dignity" in the Chinese Constitution have a strong connection to the protection of privacy rights and the

1. 参见张翔:《基本权利的规范建构》，高等教育出版社2008年版，第120 - 121页*See* Zhang Xiang, "Normative Construction of Basic Rights," (Higher Education Press 2008 edition), pp. 120–121.

preservation of personal information. The "human rights clause" provided in Article 33 of the Constitution can function as the normative foundation for "unenumerated fundamental rights" or "general freedom of action." The need to recognize "unenumerated fundamental rights" is grounded in the requirement for the constitution to remain interpretively flexible, as there is a natural friction between the codified legal texts of civil law nations and the evolution of society.[2] The right to privacy embodies elements of safeguarding human rights, and the notion of "unenumerated fundamental rights" offers a potential avenue for interpreting the right to privacy within a constitutional framework.

21. The commonly held view posits that the personal dignity safeguarded by Article 38 of the Constitution is classified among fundamental rights that cannot be legally curtailed, encompassing the right to privacy.[3] This general personality right in the Constitution is connected with the general personality right in civil law, both aiming to protect unenumerated personality rights. Article 38 of the Constitution adopts an approach of general dignity coupled with specific enumerations. However, providing specific content doesn't constrain the broad application of personality rights in civil law. On the one hand, the Constitution, as the paramount law in China, directs the establishment of an internal structure of constitutional order through various departmental laws. Any measure taken to protect privacy at any level fundamentally aims to preserve the most essential freedoms and dignity as enshrined in the Constitution. On the other hand, the interpretive latitude of the Constitution can be fully utilized to expand the understanding of the term "any," thus creating an environment conducive to fulfilling the legislative goal of preserving the dignity of citizens.[4]

22. "According to the Constitution" is a normative statement, which means that different forms of basic interests are derived from the personal dignity clause in Article 38 of the Constitution. Also, the provision of general personality rights stipulated in the Civil Code is the result of civil legislators implementing the state's obligation to protect fundamental rights. It acts as a receptor, dealing with areas that specific personality rights cannot protect.[5] With the ever-changing threats caused by information technology, the general personality right is poised to become the trump card in the future evolution of information privacy rights in China. Maintaining the alignment of general personality rights between the Constitution and civil law is crucial because it highlights the binding force that constitutional provisions have on

---

2. 参见李忠夏：《数字时代隐私权的宪法建构》，载《华东政法大学学报》2021年第3期，第46页。*See* Li Zhongxia, "Constitutional Construction of Privacy Rights in the Digital Age," published in "Journal of East China University of Political Science and Law," 3 (2021), p. 46.
3. 参见胡锦光、韩大元：《中国宪法》，法律出版社2007年版，第280页。*See* Hu Jinguang & Han Dayuan, "Chinese Constitution," (Law Press 2007 edition), p. 280.
4. 参见郑贤君：《宪法 "人格尊严" 条款的规范地位之辩》，载《中国法学》2012年的2期，第87 – 88页。*See* Zheng Xianjun, "Debate on the Normative Status of the 'Personal Dignity' Clause in the Constitution," published in "China Law Review," 2 (2012), pp. 87–88.
5. 王锴：《论宪法上的一般人格权及其对民法的影响》，载《中国法学》2017年第3期，第102 – 103页。Wang Kai, "On the General Personality Rights in the Constitution and Its Impact on Civil Law," published in "China Law Review," 3 (2017), pp. 102–103.

legislative bodies. The Chinese Constitution has never been a basic law solely to restrain state power; private rights have always been in the vision of the constitution-makers. Under the Chinese Constitution, the state has an obligation to protect citizens' fundamental rights from infringement by other private parties, and it should take appropriate measures to prevent harm to legal interests.[6] This serves as a significant constitutional foundation for concurrently curbing the powers related to information, both public and private.

23. In the Chinese Constitution, although privacy is not explicitly stipulated, it is scattered throughout different constitutional clauses. In addition to establishing the right to privacy from the perspective of "unenumerated fundamental rights," it is also necessary to normatively construct the right to privacy from the perspective of the constitutional system. For instance, Article 39's "inviolability of the residence" and Article 40's "freedom and confidentiality of correspondence" in the Constitution each cover the private space in privacy and information privacy in communication, respectively. Other facets of privacy, such as the self-determination of personal matters, private information beyond communication, and other personal information, should be protected under the "general privacy right," which can be derived from the "personal dignity clause" in Article 38, in conjunction with the "human rights clause" in Article 33 of the Constitution. Furthermore, the aforementioned clauses stipulate various degrees of restrictive provisions in their text. For "freedom and confidentiality of correspondence," the text sets a kind of "aggravated legal reservation." As for the "inviolability of the residence," the text adopts the simple legal reservation, and its restrictions are only limited to "search and intrusion." Regarding the "general right to privacy," if any interference involves circumstances like "insult," "defamation," "framing," and the like, it should be strictly prohibited. Apart from this, it is enough to meet the requirements of simple legal reservation. In addition, apart from the special restrictions on residences and correspondence stipulated in the Constitution, a general restriction as per Article 51 of the Constitution should be applied to the general right to privacy.

24. The rapid development of European privacy law benefits from its clear positioning in the Constitution. Currently, the reconstruction of China's information privacy law system urgently needs to find its roots at the constitutional level. With the basic goal of safeguarding information rights and controlling the abuse of information power, it is necessary to establish a comprehensive framework for the civil, criminal, and special law protection of information privacy per the Constitution.[7] It is important to note that the constitutionalization of information privacy is not just a matter of simply enshrining the right to privacy at the constitutional level. More crucially, it involves establishing the fundamental goal and positioning for the protection of information privacy based on the evolution of constitutional mechanism.

6. 参见陈征：《基本权利的国家保护义务功能》，载《法学研究》2008年第1期，第52页。*See* Chen Zheng, "The State's Duty to Protect Basic Rights," published in "Legal Studies," 1 (2008), p. 52.
7. 参见李海平：《基本权利客观价值秩序理论的反思与重构》，《中外法学》2020年第4期，第1063页。*See* Li Haiping, "Reflection and Reconstruction of the Theory on the Objective Value Order of Basic Rights," published in "Chinese and Foreign Law," 4 (2020), p. 1063.

§2. Privacy Rights in the Civil Code

25. Due to influences such as societal structure, cultural traditions, and lagging legal development, privacy rights have remained concealed in the legislative process of Chinese civil law. However, subsequent judicial interpretations played a significant role in promoting the development of privacy rights. Ultimately, civil law legislation affirmed and recognized privacy rights, which have gradually become the strongest and most extensive basis for judicial decisions related to privacy cases. In 2009, China launched the Tort Liability Law, which explicitly defined privacy rights as a specific personality right. In 2020, China enacted the Civil Code, which provides more comprehensive provisions on privacy rights. Article 1032 of the Civil code explicitly outlines the content and definition of privacy rights, stating that individuals possess the right to privacy. Specifically, the right to privacy includes the right to privacy possession, privacy protection, privacy disclosure, among others. For the first time, privacy was explicitly defined, referring to "the personal tranquility in private life and the private space, activities, and information that individuals do not wish to be known by others."[8]

26. The term "personal tranquility in private life" refers to the right of individuals to exclude unwarranted disturbances and interferences by others that disrupt their peaceful and stable living conditions.[9] The phrase "private space, activities, and information that individuals do not wish to be known by others" refers to the fulfillment of two subjective and objective requirements of "do not wish to be known by others" and "being in an undisclosed state," which applies to the dimensions of space, activities, and information. The phrase "do not wish to be known by others" refers to the subjective intent of individuals. However, the subjective intent of individuals should not be solely determined by their own will; it should be based on the premise of generally reasonable understanding. The second part, "being in an undisclosed state," refers to an objective status of the space, activities, and information. Private space not only includes physical spaces such as residences and hotel rooms but also virtual spaces such as email inboxes and WeChat groups. Private activities refer to personal activities conducted by individuals that are unrelated to the public interest, such as daily life, family activities, marital activities, and sexual activities. Private information refers to information that is closely related to the individual, highly private, and which the individual is extremely unwilling to expose to the public view, such as medical records, financial records, and sexual orientation information. Article 1033 lists the main behaviors that infringe upon others' privacy rights and uses "infringement on others' privacy rights in other ways" as a catch-all clause. Also, the Civil Code provides for the right to claim personality rights[10] and

8. Article 1032 of the Civil Code of the People's Republic of China.
9. 王利明：《人格权法研究》，中国人民大学出版社2018年版，第590页。Wang Liming, "Research on Personality Rights Law," (Renmin University Press 2018 edition), p. 590.
10. Article 995 of the "Civil Code" stipulates that when personality rights are infringed upon, the victim has the right, in accordance with this law and other legal provisions, to request the actor to bear civil liability. In addition, Arts. 997, 998, and 1000 of the "Civil Code" provide systematic regulations on the right to claim personality rights, which are applicable to the protection of privacy rights.

the right to claim compensation for tort damages.[11] These provisions form a comprehensive framework for privacy protection, which will act as a crucial legal foundation for future standards of judgment and behavior norms related to privacy in China.

§3. Protection of Privacy by Other Laws and Regulations

27. The "General Principles of Civil Law" enacted and promulgated by China in 1986 is an important milestone in civil legislation after the establishment of the People's Republic of China. However, it is regrettable that it only stipulates the protection of rights such as the right to life and health, the right to a name, the right to a portrait, the right to reputation, and the right to honor, etc. The right to privacy is not included in these stipulations. Therefore, at most, we can consider that the right to privacy is implicitly covered under "etc." In 1988, the Supreme People's Court issued the "Opinions on Several Issues Concerning the Implementation of the General Principles of the Civil Law of the People's Republic of China (Trial)." Its Article 140 stipulates: "Publicizing others' privacy in written or oral form, or fabricating facts to publicly defame others' personalities, as well as damaging others' reputation by means of insult and slander, and causing certain impact, should be identified as behaviors infringing upon the citizen's right to reputation." Although the term "privacy" in this context might only refer to the traditional Chinese notion of private relationships between men and women, and the related "private matters," which is substantially different from the original meaning of "privacy," this has indeed become the legal foundation of privacy protection in China, that is, protecting citizens' privacy rights indirectly through the right to reputation. It can be said that it was the Supreme People's Court that filled the gap in legislation through this judicial interpretation.[12] The implementation of the "Law of the People's Republic of China on the Protection of Minors" in 1991 made up for the legislative omission of not mentioning "privacy" in the law.[13] The concept of "privacy rights" was further introduced into legislative documents not on the civil law level but in the "Law of the People's Republic of China on the Protection of Women's Rights and Interests" revised in 2005, which is a kind of social law.[14] It wasn't until the "Tort Liability Law" in 2009 that China clearly stipulated the right to privacy in its basic civil

11. Article 1165 of the "Civil Code" stipulates the general tort liability. If a person, due to negligence, infringes upon others' civil rights and interests and causes damage, he or she shall bear the tort liability. This provision is also applicable to privacy rights.
12. A typical case from that time is the case of Lotus Girl. The defendant wrote a novel based on the late artist "Lotus Lady." The novel includes fictional content and illustrations that tarnish the reputation of the deceased. The plaintiff (the mother of "Lotus Lady") filed a lawsuit against the defendant, alleging that the defendant violated the reputation rights of both the deceased and herself.
13. Article 30 of the "Protection of Minors Act of the People's Republic of China," promulgated in September 1991 (now obsolete), stipulates: "No organization or individual shall disclose the personal privacy of minors."
14. Article 42 of the "Law on the Protection of Women's Rights and Interests of the People's Republic of China," stipulates: "Women's rights to reputation, honor, privacy, and portrait, among other personal rights, are protected by law."

law and classified it as a specific personality right. Since then, the statutory attribute of the right to privacy has been officially recognized at the level of civil legislation in China.

28. However, before the introduction of the "Civil Code" in 2020, China had not yet established a systematic and comprehensive privacy protection legislation and instead was in a state of protection characterized by scattered legislation. They include such individual laws as the "Consumer Rights Protection Law" (2013), "Cybersecurity Law" (2016), "General Principles of Civil Law" (2017), "E-Commerce Law" (2018); administrative regulations such as the "Decision of the Standing Committee of National People's Congress on Strengthening Network Information Protection" (2012), criminal laws such as the "Seventh Amendment to the Criminal Law" (2009) and "Ninth Amendment to the Criminal Law" (2015), and judicial interpretations issued by the Supreme People's Court and the Supreme People's Procuratorate such as the "Provisions on Several Issues Concerning the Application of Law in Civil Dispute Cases Involving Infringement of Personal Rights and Interests by Use of Information Networks" (2014), "Interpretation on Several Issues Concerning the Application of Law in Criminal Cases of Infringement of Citizens' Personal Information" (2017). In addition, specific industries often introduce industry standards before legislation to protect personal information in their fields. For instance, the finance industry has issued the "Regulations on the Management of the Credit Industry" (2013) and "Technical Standards for the Protection of Personal Financial Information" (2020), among others; the medical industry has launched the "Information Security Technology: Health and Medical Information Security Guidelines" (2021), "Interim Measures for the Management of Human Genetic Resources" (2019) and etc.

29. Currently, a relatively complete legal system for the protection of privacy rights has been established. In addition to the "Constitution" and the "Civil Code," there are several other important laws and regulations, such as the "Cybersecurity Law" and the "Data Security Law." It can be seen that the development of privacy rights protection has now extended from the field of civil law to a wider range of other sectoral law fields. For example, Article 45 of the "Cybersecurity Law" stipulates the confidentiality obligations of departments and their staff responsible for network security supervision and management. It states that "departments and their staff who are legally responsible for network security supervision and management must strictly maintain confidentiality of personal information, privacy, and commercial secrets that they come to know in the course of performing their duties. They must not disclose, sell, or unlawfully provide them to others." Also, Article 38 of the "Data Security Law" stipulates the obligations of state organs to protect privacy when collecting and using data. It states that "state organs should collect and use data within the scope of their statutory duties and in accordance with the conditions and procedures stipulated by law and administrative regulations when it is necessary to fulfill their statutory duties. They should legally maintain confidentiality of data such as personal privacy, personal information, commercial secrets, and confidential business information that they come to know in the course of performing their duties. They must not disclose or unlawfully provide them to others."

§4. DIFFERENTIATION BETWEEN PRIVACY AND PERSONAL INFORMATION

30. Article 1034 of the "Civil Code" stipulates that "the personal information of a natural person is protected by law. Personal information is various information recorded electronically or in other ways, that can identify a specific natural person alone or in combination with other information, including a natural person's name, date of birth, identity document number, biometric information, residential address, telephone number, email address, health information, whereabouts, and the like. For private information in personal information, the provisions related to privacy rights apply; if non-private information in personal information, the provisions related to the protection of personal information apply."

31. Many Chinese scholars believe that the rights to privacy and personal information are two independent specific personality rights, and neither can replace or include the other. In fact, Chinese law also pays attention to the distinction between privacy and personal information. As early as December 2012, the Standing Committee of the National People's Congress issued the "Decision on Strengthening Network Information Protection," in which the first paragraph of Article 1 distinguishes electronic information into electronic information that can identify the personal identity of citizens (i.e., personal information) and electronic information that involves the personal privacy of citizens (i.e., privacy).

32. In subsequent legislation including the "Cybersecurity Law," "E-commerce Law," "Counter-Terrorism Law," and "Criminal Procedure Law," the lawmakers concurrently regulated personal information and privacy, thereby providing distinct protection to each. For example, Article 25 of the "E-commerce Law" stipulates: "The relevant competent departments should take necessary measures to protect the data information provided by e-commerce operators, and strictly keep the personal information, privacy, and commercial secrets therein confidential, and they shall not disclose, sell, or illegally provide them to others." Article 45 of the "Cybersecurity Law" stipulates: "Departments and their staff who are legally responsible for network security supervision and management must strictly maintain confidentiality of personal information, privacy, and commercial secrets that they come to know in the course of performing their duties. They must not disclose, sell, or unlawfully provide them to others."

33. The "General Principles of Civil Law" promulgated in 2017 stipulated specific personality rights such as privacy rights (Article 110) and also made specific provisions for the protection of personal information (Article 111), which have now become Articles 110 and 111 of the "Civil Code." The "Civil Code" has also made provisions for "privacy rights and personal information protection" in a dedicated chapter (Chapter 6) in the compilation of personality rights. Despite the cautious considerations of the legislature, in order to "avoid unnecessary misunderstandings, and prevent hindrance to data sharing, data utilization and the development of the big data industry in China,"[15] the concept of "personal information rights" was not adopted in the "Civil Code," and only a more general expression, "personal information protection" was used. Despite the prudence of the legislative body to "avoid unnecessary misinterpretations, and to prevent obstacles to data sharing, utilization, and the growth of the big data industry in China," they did not use the term "personal information rights" in the "Civil Code." Instead, they opted for a broader phrase, namely "personal information protection." However, since the "Civil Code" combines the provisions of "personal information protection" with privacy rights in the compilation of personality rights, this clearly indicates that privacy rights and personal information are two parallel types of personality rights.

34. Ten months after the implementation of the "Civil Code," the "Personal Information Protection Law" was enacted. This law goes even further on the basis of the "Civil Code," and, for the first time, proposes the concept of "personal information rights and interests." Article 1 of the "Personal Information Protection Law" takes "protecting personal information rights and interests" as the primary legislative purpose. Meanwhile, Article 2 stipulates that "the personal information of natural persons is protected by law, and no organization or individual may infringe upon the personal information rights and interests of natural persons." In addition, Article 69 makes specific provisions for the attribution principles of tort liability and the calculation method of damage compensation when the processor infringes upon personal information rights and interests and causes damage.

35. Prior to the introduction of the "Civil Code," legal protections for personal information were commonly placed under the umbrella of privacy rights during judicial proceedings. As a result, several instances of personal information that didn't align with privacy criteria weren't adequately safeguarded. With the promulgation of the "Civil Code" and "Personal Information Protection Law," privacy rights and personal information rights and interests as two coexisting rights have been clearly defined in Chinese laws. A paradigm of judicial precedents that makes a distinction between the protections of these two rights is the case of "WeChat Reading,"[16] which is emblematic of personal information privacy violations in the aftermath of the "Civil Code's" enactment. In this case, the court concluded that the reading information of the plaintiff didn't meet the standard of confidentiality; thus,

15. 黄薇主编：《中华人民共和国民法典人格权编解读》，中国法制出版社2020年版，第213页。Huang Wei (edi.), "Interpretation of the Personality Rights Section of the Civil Code of the People's Republic of China," (China Legal Publishing House 2020 edition), p. 213.
16. WeChat Reading is a mobile reading application where users can read books, share book reviews, etc. WeChat is a mobile social application where users can add friends, instant message, and perform other operations. The plaintiff, Huang, discovered that due to WeChat sharing its friend data with WeChat Reading, the names of Huang's WeChat friends who use WeChat Reading appeared under the "Follow" column in WeChat Reading. Furthermore, WeChat Reading automatically displayed information such as the books Huang was reading, thoughts on the books, and Huang's bookshelf to both friends who followed Huang and those who didn't. Thus, Huang believed that these actions infringed upon his privacy rights and personal information rights. Huang demanded Tencent Computer Systems Co., Ltd. in Shenzhen (the operator of both WeChat and WeChat Reading), Tencent Technology (Shenzhen) Co., Ltd. (developer of WeChat Reading), and Tencent Technology

the defendant did not infringe on the plaintiff's privacy rights. However, the actions of WeChat Reading –collecting the list of the plaintiff's WeChat friends, automatically revealing the plaintiff's reading information to WeChat friends who weren't actively added by the plaintiff, and failing to provide a reasonable level of "transparency" or obtaining the plaintiff's consent –were ruled as infringements of the plaintiff's rights to personal information.

36. The distinction between privacy rights and personal information protection mainly lies in the differences in the attributes of their respective objects. Privacy rights solely carry personality interests, while personal information in the context of the big data era involves personality interests, property interests, and public interests.[17] As for personal information, individuals often have the willingness to trade subjectively, hoping others know or don't care if others know. Objectively, due to the practical needs of participating in social life, their personal information can be utilized by others. In contrast, while privacy also pertains to personality interests, individuals subjectively do not wish their private information to be revealed, and objectively, privacy cannot be freely exchanged or disposed of at will.[18] Considering the similarities and differences between the attributes of privacy and personal information, both the "Civil Code" and the "Personal Information Protection Law" adopt the concept of "personal information rights and interests," reflecting the goal of striking a balance between competing interests. On one hand, they have to protect the legitimate interests of the subject of personal information and prevent harm to the dignity of the subject. On the other hand, they intend to avoid providing absolute protection for personal information, which may hinder the reasonable use of personal information.

37. Both privacy rights and personal information are specific types of personality rights and interests. Privacy emphasizes confidentiality in a narrow sense, while personal information emphasizes external identifiability. Compared to traditional personality rights, personal information not only embodies personal interests but also includes property interests.[19] Preservation of personal information doesn't just center around protecting the personality interests related to personal information, but also takes into account the objective requirements of the digital economy's evolution, while guarding the inherent property interests. The externalization and

(Beijing) Co., Ltd. (developer of WeChat) to cease the infringement and issue an apology, among other remedies. Reference: Beijing Internet Court, Civil Judgement (2019) Jing 0491 Civil Initial 16142.

17. 参见姬蕾蕾：《企业数据保护的司法困境与破局之维：类型化确权之路》，载《法学论坛》2022年第3期，第113页。*See* Ji Leilei, "The Judicial Dilemma and Way Out for Corporate Data Protection: The Path of Typified Rights Confirmation," published in "Legal Studies Forum," 3 (2022), p. 113.
18. 参见彭诚信、杨思益：《论数据、信息与隐私的权利层次与体系建构》，载《西北工业大学学报》2020年第2期，第81页。*See* Peng Chengxin & Yang Siyi, "On the Hierarchies and System Construction of Data, Information, and Privacy Rights," published in "Journal of Northwestern Polytechnical University," 2 (2020), p. 81.
19. 参见向秦、高富平：《论个人信息权益的财产属性》，载《南京社会科学》2022年第2期，第92页。*See* Xiang Qin & Gao Fuping, "On the Property Attributes of Personal Information Rights," in "Nanjing Social Sciences," 2 (2022), p. 92.

utilization of personal information as a property must always be subject to the legal restriction that its personality interest is not violated. That is, the protection of personality rights and interests of personal information is a necessary condition and baseline for data generation and utilization.[20]

20. 参见彭诚信：《论个人信息的双重法律属性》，载《清华法学》2021年第6期，第93页。*See* Peng Chengxin, "On the Dual Legal Attributes of Personal Information," in "Tsinghua Law Journal," 6 (2021), p. 93.

Part II. Personal Information Protection Legislation

§1. Legislative Background

38. With the continuous development of the Internet, incidents of infringement of personal information occur frequently. In order to protect the lawful rights and interests of the subject of personal information, China has explicitly stipulated rules for the protection of personal information in many normative documents. Since the Standing Committee of the National People's Congress issued the "Decision on Strengthening the Protection of Online Information" in 2012, China began to build a personal information protection system featuring individual control. The "Consumer Rights Protection Law" amended in 2013, the "Cybersecurity Law" passed in 2016, and the "E-commerce Law" passed in 2018 all include specific provisions for the protection of personal information. The Seventh Amendment to the Criminal Law passed in 2009 added Article 253-1, which established two crimes of "selling or illegally providing citizen's personal information" and "illegally obtaining citizen's personal information." The Ninth Amendment to the Criminal Law passed in 2015 consolidated these two crimes into one: "the violation of citizen's personal information" and further improved the specific rules, such as expanding the scope of offenders and raising the legal punishment, which can effectively crack down on criminal acts infringing on citizens' personal information. Article 111 of the "General Provisions of the Civil Law" passed in 2017 stipulates: "The personal information of natural persons is protected by law. Any organization or individual that needs to obtain others' personal information must obtain it in accordance with the law and ensure the security of the information. They may not illegally collect, use, process, transmit, buy, sell, provide or disclose others' personal information."

39. The "Civil Code" passed in 2020 retains Article 111 of the "General Provisions of the Civil Law" and further stipulates specific rules for the protection of personal information. Specifically, Chapter 6, "Privacy Rights and Personal Information Protection" of the "Civil Code," includes six provisions that directly involve the specific rules of personal information protection, covering important aspects such as the definition of personal information, the legal basis for personal information processing, and the rights of personal information subjects, thereby establishing the core content of personal information protection. Following the enactment of the "Civil Code," China expedited the drafting of the "Personal Information Protection Law," which was officially promulgated in August 2021. This law, comprising eight chapters and seventy-four articles, encompasses important aspects such as the definition of personal information, fundamental principles of personal information processing, specific rules for personal information processing, individuals' rights during personal information processing activities, obligations of personal information processors, the departments responsible for fulfilling personal information protection duties, and the legal responsibilities for unlawful processing of personal information. This changes the longstanding situation in China where personal information was protected through dispersed legislation. It builds up a systematic and comprehensive legal framework for the personal information protection system, marking the substantial development of China's legal system in the realm of personal information protection.

§2. The Scope of Application

40. Article 3 of the "Personal Information Protection Law" clearly defines the application scope of this law, stating that "activities that process the personal information of natural persons within the territory of the People's Republic of China shall be governed by this Law." This provision includes the following key points. First, the application of China's "Personal Information Protection Law" is based on the principle of territorial jurisdiction. Regardless of whether the processor is an organization or an individual, and regardless of whether the processor is a Chinese citizen or organization, as long as they process the personal information of natural persons within the territory of the People's Republic of China, they will be subject to the regulation of this law. Second, the "Personal Information Protection Law" regulates the activities of processing personal information of natural persons rather than regulating activities processing information of legal persons or non-legal person organizations. The law confines the scope of the subject of personal information to natural persons, and Article 2 stipulates: "The personal information of natural persons is protected by law, and no organization or individual may infringe upon the rights and interests of personal information of natural persons." Third, The "Personal Information Protection Law" is designed to safeguard the personal information of natural persons, that is, "various information related to an identified or identifiable natural person as recorded electronically or via other means," as defined by Article 4. This law does not apply to "non-personal information." Fourth, regarding the types of activities processing personal information of natural persons, Article 4, paragraph 2 of the "Personal Information Protection Law" stipulates: "The processing of personal information includes the collection, storage, use, processing, transmission, provision, disclosure, and deletion of personal information." Different from Article 1035, paragraph 2 of the "Civil Code," Article 4, paragraph 2 of the "Personal Information Protection Law" clearly states that "deletion" is also considered personal information processing activity.

41. With the continuous deepening of economic globalization, the personal information of natural persons in China may be transmitted abroad and processed by foreign organizations or individuals. Therefore, to protect the rights and interests of the personal information of natural persons within China, Article 3, paragraph 2 of the "Personal Information Protection Law" clearly states that activities processing personal information of natural persons within the territory of the People's Republic of China from abroad are also subject to regulation under the "Personal Information Protection Law" under specific circumstances. This provision explicitly lists two scenarios, namely, processing with the aim of providing products or services to natural persons within the territory and analyzing and evaluating the behavior of natural persons within the territory. In addition, this provision also includes a catch-all clause, "other circumstances prescribed by laws and administrative regulations," to cover any instances not specifically listed above, thereby ensuring complete protection of the personal information rights and interests of natural persons within the territory of China. Also, Article 72, paragraph 1 of the "Personal Information Protection Law" stipulates: "This Law does not apply to the processing of personal information by natural persons for personal or household affairs." This provision clearly states that such personal information processing activities are not within the scope of the "Personal Information Protection Law," implying that natural persons who process personal information for personal or household affairs are not considered personal information processors as stipulated in Article 73, paragraph 1 of the law, and therefore are not subject to its regulation. However, it is important to emphasize that the processing of personal information by natural persons for personal or household affairs is not free from legal regulation. If such personal information processing activities infringe on others' rights and interests, they can be regulated by such provisions as the right to reputation and right to privacy in the "Civil Code." In addition, Article 72, paragraph 2 of the "Personal Information Protection Law" stipulates: "Where laws have provisions on the processing of personal information in the statistical and archival management activities organized by people's governments at all levels and their relevant departments, such provisions shall apply." In other words, the activities of statistics and archive management have obvious uniqueness, so they should primarily comply with the provisions of relevant laws such as the "Statistics Law" and the "Archives Law." If there are no relevant regulations, then the "Personal Information Protection Law" should be applied.

§3. Concepts and Definitions

42. Personal information is the core concept in the legal system of personal information protection, and it directly affects the scope of personal information protection. As to what constitutes personal information, various normative documents in China provide clear definitions. For example, Article 76, paragraph 5 of the "Cybersecurity Law" stipulates: "Personal information refers to various information that can identify the personal identity of a natural person alone or in combination with other information, as recorded electronically or by other means, including but not limited to the name, date of birth, identification document number, personal biometric information, residential address, telephone number, and the like of the person." This provision clearly adopts "identifiability of the personal identity" as the criterion for judging personal information.[21] Article 1034, paragraph 2 of the "Civil Code" stipulates: "Personal information is various information that can identify a specific natural person alone or in combination with other information, as recorded electronically or by other means, including the name, date of birth, identity document number, biometric information, residential address, telephone number, email address, health information, whereabouts, and the like of the person." Different from Article 76, paragraph 5 of the "Cybersecurity Law," Article 1034, paragraph 2 of the "Civil Code" adopts a broad "identifiability of the person" standard to judge personal information, rather than being limited to "identifiability of the personal identity."

43. Compared with the "Cybersecurity Law" and the "Civil Code," the "Personal Information Protection Law" adopts a different standard for determining personal information. Article 4, paragraph 1 of the law stipulates: "Personal information refers to various pieces of information related to an identified or identifiable natural person, which is recorded electronically or by other means, excluding information after anonymization." First, this provision adopts "relevance" as the criterion for judging personal information, while Article 76, paragraph 5 of the "Cybersecurity Law" and Article 1034, paragraph 2 of the "Civil Code" both use "identifiability" as the criterion for determining personal information. Second, while defining personal information, Article 76, paragraph 5 of the "Cybersecurity Law" and Article 1034, paragraph 2 of the "Civil Code" explicitly specify common types of personal information in a listing manner. However, Article 4, paragraph 1 of the "Personal Information Protection Law" does not adopt this enumerative approach but instead uses an exclusionary method, clarifying that information processed through anonymization does not constitute personal information. The "Personal Information Protection Law" also defines sensitive personal information. According to paragraph 1 of Article 28: "Sensitive personal information refers to personal information that, if leaked or illegally used, can easily infringe upon a natural person's dignity, or endanger their personal and property safety. This includes information on biometric identification, religious beliefs, specific identity, medical health, financial accounts, and personal whereabouts among others, as well as personal information of minors under fourteen years old." This provision uses a "definition + enumeration" method to define sensitive personal information. It differentiates personal information into sensitive and non-sensitive personal information, allowing the "Personal Information Protection Law" to establish specific protection rules for sensitive personal information.

44. The "Personal Information Protection Law" specifically defines four concepts: personal information processors, automated decision-making, de-identification, and anonymization. Article 73, paragraph 1 states: "Personal

---

21. 参见彭诚信、史晓宇：《个人信息识别标准的域外考察和在中国的转进——基于美欧国家制度互动的分析》，载《河南社会科学》2020年第11期，第2页。*See* Peng Chengxin & Shi Xiaoyu, "An Overseas Examination of Personal Information Identification Standards and Its Transition in China—An Analysis Based on the Interaction of US-European Systems," in "Henan Social Sciences," 11 (2020), p. 2.

information processor refers to an organization or individual who independently decides on the processing purpose and processing methods during personal information processing activities." First, personal information processors include not only organizations but also individuals. Although, in practice, personal information processors are typically organizations, it should not be denied that individuals can also become personal information processors. Second, a key characteristic of personal information processors is the ability to independently determine the purpose and method of processing. If an organization or individual processes personal information based on the purpose and method determined by others, they do not fall under the definition of personal information processors. According to Article 73, paragraph 2 of the "Personal Information Protection Law," "automated decision-making refers to the activity of analyzing and evaluating an individual's behavioral habits, interests, economic, health, credit status, among others, through computer programs, and making decisions." In simple terms, automated decision-making is the process in which computer programs replace traditional human labor to conduct analysis, evaluation, and make decisions. Automated decision-making consists of two stages. First, based on the collection of personal information, a digital profile of the individual is created. Through computer programs, the individual's behavioral habits, interests, economic, health, credit status, and other characteristics are automatically analyzed and evaluated. These analysis and evaluation activities fall under personal information processing activities. Second, the decision-making process is carried out based on the outcomes of the analysis and evaluation, such as delivering targeted advertisements. According to Article 73, paragraph 3 of the "Personal Information Protection Law," de-identification refers to the process of processing personal information in a way that it cannot identify a specific individual without additional information. There is a significant distinction between de-identification and anonymization of personal information. De-identified information cannot directly identify a specific individual but can still be combined with other information to achieve the identification of a specific individual. Therefore, de-identified information is still considered personal information and should be subject to the relevant provisions of the "Personal Information Protection Law." In comparison, anonymized information provides a higher level of protection in terms of the inability to identify a specific individual. As stated in Article 73, paragraph 4 of the "Personal Information Protection Law," anonymization refers to the process of processing personal information in a way that it cannot identify a specific individual and cannot be restored. The commonality between anonymization and de-identification lies in the fact that both processes render personal information unable to identify a specific individual. However, the distinction is that anonymized information cannot be technically restored to achieve re-identification of a specific individual. Therefore, Article 4, paragraph 1 of the "Personal Information Protection Law" explicitly states that anonymized information is not considered personal information and is not subject to the relevant provisions of the law. For instance, the processing of such information does not require obtaining the individual's consent.

45. "The Cybersecurity Law" not only clearly defines the meaning of personal information but also clarifies the specific meanings of concepts such as networks, cybersecurity, network operators, and network data. Article 76, paragraph 1 of the

"Cybersecurity Law" stipulates: "A network refers to a system composed of computers or other information terminals and related equipment that collect, store, transmit, exchange, and process information in accordance with certain rules and procedures." The term "network" in this provision refers to a broad sense of network, which not only includes the Internet, but also relatively closed local area networks and industrial control systems. This way of defining is in line with the reality of China's cybersecurity management work.[22]

46. Article 76, paragraph 2 of the law stipulates: "Cybersecurity refers to the adoption of necessary measures to prevent attacks, intrusions, interference, destruction, and illegal use of networks, as well as unexpected accidents, to keep the network in a stable and reliable operating state, and to ensure the integrity, confidentiality, and availability of network data." The cybersecurity defined in this provision includes both the safety of network operations and the safety of network data. Network operation safety refers to the normal operation of the network technology system, free from illegal operations and attacks. This includes the safety of network infrastructure operations, platform operations, and user network operations, etc. It mainly manifests as technical confrontations between network users, and its solutions mainly lie in the upgrading of cybersecurity protection measures and the improvement of internal management.[23] The integrity, confidentiality, and availability of network data are the goals of network data security, and the mechanism to ensure network data security is to prohibit unauthorized access, use, disclosure, destruction, modification, or deletion.[24] A core concept closely related to networks and cybersecurity is the network operator, which is the main regulatory object of the "Cybersecurity Law." Article 76, paragraph 3 of the "Cybersecurity Law" stipulates: "Network operators refer to network owners, managers, and network service providers." It can be seen that the scope of network operators here is quite broad, not only including common network service providers, but also the owners and managers of the network. Article 76, paragraph 4 of the law stipulates: "Network data refers to various electronic data collected, stored, transmitted, processed, and generated through the network." The so-called network data is essentially an electronic form of information. The network data here is different from the "data" stipulated in Article 3, paragraph 1 of the "Data Security Law." This paragraph stipulates: "Data refers to any record of information in electronic or other forms." Obviously, although the "data" stipulated by the "Data Security Law" is a record of information, it is not limited to the electronic form and has a broader scope.

---

22. 参见杨合庆主编：《<中华人民共和国网络安全法>释义》，中国民主法制出版社2016年版，第150－151页。*See* Yang Heqing (Editor-in-chief), "Interpretation of the Cybersecurity Law of the People's Republic of China," (China Democracy and Legal System Publishing House 2016 edition), pp. 150–151.

23. 参见梅夏英：《信息和数据概念区分的法律意义》，载《比较法研究》2020年第6期，第157页。Mei Xiaying, "The Legal Significance of Distinguishing between Information and Data Concepts," in "Comparative Law Research," 6 (2020), p. 157.

24. 参见翟志勇：《数据安全法的体系定位》，载《苏州大学学报(哲学社会科学版)》2021年第1期，第77页。Zhai Zhiyong, "The Systematic Positioning of the Data Security Law," in "Journal of Suzhou University (Philosophy and Social Sciences Edition)," 1 (2021), p. 77.

Part III. Principles of Personal Information Protection

§1. General Principles of Personal Information Protection

47. The "Decision of the Standing Committee of the National People's Congress on Strengthening the Protection of Network Information" (2012) stipulates that "Internet service providers and other entities shall, when collecting and using citizens' electronic personal information in business activities, adhere to the principles of legality, legitimacy and necessity, explicitly state the purposes, manners and scopes of collecting and using information, and obtain the consent of those from whom information is collected, and shall not collect and use information in violation of laws and regulations and the agreement between both sides; Internet service providers and other entities shall, when collecting and using citizens' electronic personal information, publish their collection and use rules." This provision has factually established four principles for processing personal information, namely, legality, legitimacy, necessity, and openness. Along the same line, the first paragraph of Article 41 in the "Cybersecurity Law" provides that "network operators collecting and using personal information shall abide by the principles of legality, legitimacy, and necessity, disclosing their rules for its collection and use, explicitly stating the purposes, means and scope for collecting or using information, and obtaining the consent of the person whose data is gathered." The first paragraph of Article 1035 in the Civil Code also provides that "the processing of personal information shall be in compliance with the principles of legality, legitimacy, and necessity, and shall not be excessively processed." In the process of formulating the "Personal Information Protection Law," Chinese legislative authorities believed that the basic principles of personal information processing should be further improved on the basis of such laws as the "Civil Code" and "Cybersecurity Law." Therefore, Articles 5 to 9 of this law respectively stipulate the principles of legality, legitimacy, necessity, and good faith, the principle of purpose limitation, principles of openness and transparency, principle of quality, and principles of accountability and security.

I. Principles of Legality, Legitimacy, Necessity, and Good Faith

48. Article 5 of the "Personal Information Protection Law" stipulates that "the processing of personal information should adhere to the principles of legality, legitimacy, necessity, and good faith, and personal information should not be processed by means of deception, fraud, coercion, etc." The principle of legality is the first fundamental principle that must be followed when processing personal information, which includes legality of purpose, legality of cause, and legality of action. When individuals or entities process personal information, including activities such as collecting, storing, processing, using, providing, and publishing, they should strictly adhere to legal provisions and adopt lawful methods. Any unlawful processing of personal information is prohibited. The underlying assumption of the principle of legality is that any processing of personal information is objectively an infringement or disruption of a natural person's privacy rights and interests. Therefore, such processing must be based on legal grounds or justifiable reasons. Otherwise, it would be considered illegal and infringing on personal information rights and interests. In the Chinese legal system, the "law" in "legality" has a wide scope, including laws enacted by the National People's Congress and its Standing Committee, administrative regulations, local regulations, judicial interpretations, departmental rules, local government regulations, and mandatory national standards. The first level is the legality of purpose. That is, to pursue lawful interests without infringing on an individual's personal dignity and property rights, as well as not damaging public or national interests. For example, if the processing is for the purposes of fraud or illegal trading, sanctions would be imposed according to the "Criminal Law." The second level is the legality of cause. That is, personal information processors can only process personal information when it complies with the provisions of laws and administrative regulations. A comprehensive list of these situations can be found in Article 13 of the "Personal Information Protection Law." Any personal information processing activity must comply with one of the seven legal grounds listed in this article. For example, if the personal information processor obtains valid consent from the individual, there's no need to examine other legal grounds, unless the individual later exercises the right to revoke their consent. The third level is the legality of action. Even in situations where personal information is processed legally, such as obtaining informed and valid consent from the information subject, the processing actions should be carried out in a lawful manner, for example, fulfilling notification and reporting obligations.

49. The principle of legitimacy stipulates that the processing of personal information must be justified and should not be carried out through unjust methods, such as deception or without the individual's knowledge. This principle complements the principle of legality. In legal application, it enables the legalization of some moral standards through discretionary judgement, supplementing the obligations of personal information processors and realizing the ethical governance of personal information. When personal information processors obtain an individual's consent through fraudulent or coercive methods to process their personal information, such processing is still considered illegal according to the principle of legitimacy, and consent cannot be used as a defense. Specifically, Article 4 of the "Provisions of the

Supreme People's Court on Several Issues Concerning the Application of Law in the Trial of Civil Cases Involving the Processing of Personal Information Using Face Recognition Technology" explicitly states: "in any of the following circumstances, if the information processor argues that they have obtained the consent of the individual or their guardian, the People's Court will not support it: (1) if the information processor requires the individual's consent to process their facial information to provide products or services, unless the processing of facial information is necessary to provide the products or services; (2) if the information processor requires the individual's consent to process their facial information in conjunction with other authorizations; (3) any other circumstances where the individual is forced or indirectly forced to agree to the processing of their facial information."

50. The principle of necessity, also known as the principle of minimization, suggests that any processing of personal information should be necessary for achieving the purpose of processing. Essentially, any processing of personal information that is unnecessary should not be undertaken. This principle represents the proportionality principle in personal information protection legislation. The proportionality principle in its broad sense applies not only to public law but also to private law. For instance, in administrative law, administrative bodies are required to choose the least harmful option among various plans when it comes to the rights and interests of the administrative counterpart. In civil law, the principle of proportionality means that interference in individual freedom and private law autonomy can only occur when it is necessary to protect higher interests. Such interference should be both suitable for achieving the expected goal and the most lenient method to achieve it.[25] In terms of the "Personal Information Protection Law," the principle of necessity is mainly reflected in three aspects: (1) according to Article 6, section 2 of the law, the collection of personal information should follow the principle of necessity, limited to the minimum scope necessary to achieve the purpose of processing, and excessive collection of personal information is not permitted; (2) as per Article 28, section 2, the processing of sensitive personal information should have sufficient necessity; otherwise, such processing is not allowed; (3) as stipulated in Article 19, the retention period of personal information should be the shortest time necessary to achieve the purpose of processing, unless otherwise provided by laws and administrative regulations.

51. The principle of good faith requires that information processors should not violate the requirements of good faith when performing their obligations. The principle of good faith holds a high status in the private law system and has developed into a nearly all-encompassing, massive legal system concept. Article 7 of the "Civil Code" explicitly stipulates, "civil subjects should follow the principle of good faith, be honest, and honor their commitments when engaging in civil activities." The Personal Information Protection Law, based on the principles of "legality, legitimacy, and necessity," adds the "principle of good faith." This implies that the principle

---

25. 参见郑晓剑：《比例原则在民法上的适用及展开》，载《中国法学》2016年第2期。Zheng Xiaojian, "The Application and Development of the Proportionality Principle in Civil Law," in "China Law Science," 2 (2016).

requires parties to be honest, abide by their commitments, disclose relevant information truthfully and sincerely, not deceive others, and emphasize creditworthiness. The principle of good faith is essentially the legalization of morality. At the judicial practice level, it serves as a "blank check," granting the law discretionary power. The principle of good faith is directed at the specific exercise of rights, requiring that actions are objectively in good faith. For example, it's forbidden to process personal information through deception, fraud, coercion, etc. It also prohibits the abuse of power, random changes in conditions, and arbitrary revocations of rights, among others.

II. Principle of Purpose Limitation

52. Article 6 of the "Personal Information Protection Law" stipulates that "the processing of personal information should have a clear, reasonable purpose, and should be directly related to the processing purpose, and adopt the method that minimally impacts personal rights and interests. The collection of personal information should be limited to the smallest range necessary to achieve the processing purpose, and excessive collection of personal information is prohibited." Before the enactment of the "Personal Information Protection Law," there were no purpose limitation principles in Chinese laws including the "Cybersecurity Law" and the "Civil Code." However, the purpose limitation principle can still be interpreted from the necessity principle, as the judgment standard of necessity is precisely based on the purpose of personal information processing. This principle permeates the activities of personal information processing, and any type of processing activities carried out by any type of personal information processor are subject to this principle. As far as the Personal Information Protection Law is concerned, the purpose limitation principle has a rich connotation. First, the purpose is specific; that is, the processing of personal information should have a clear and reasonable purpose, including public interest purposes and commercial interest purposes. Second, it should be directly related to the processing purpose; that is, the processing of personal information that goes beyond the processing purpose is illegal. When the processing purpose has been achieved, cannot be achieved, or is no longer necessary for achieving the processing purpose, the personal information processor should actively delete the personal information. Third, the method that minimally impacts personal rights and interests should be adopted; that is, the personal information processor should ensure that the processing method of personal information matches the processing purpose as much as possible, the frequency of processing personal information and the degree of personal information identification should be minimized.

III. Principles of Openness and Transparency

53. Article 7 of the "Personal Information Protection Law" stipulates that "the processing of personal information should follow the principles of openness and transparency, publicize the rules of personal information processing, and clearly state the purpose, method, and scope of processing." This law uses the phrase "openness and transparency principle" for the first time, highlighting its importance as a basic principle, which has the guiding significance of a general principle and jointly safeguards the right to information and decision-making of the information subject. Article 44 of the "Personal Information Protection Law" grants natural persons the right to information and decision-making. If the personal information processor does not process personal information in an open and transparent manner but in a secretive and behind-the-scenes operation manner, then this processing behavior is infringing upon the right of the information subject to information and decision-making for their personal information, damaging their personal information rights and interests. With the development of information technology, personal information is collected and utilized automatically and rapidly. The information subject often does not know when, by whom, and how their personal information is collected and utilized. When personal information is leaked, the information subject cannot locate the source of the leak and is even less able to hold the other party legally responsible. Therefore, the principle of openness and transparency not only grants individuals the right to know about their information and hence derives their right to access and copy their personal information from the personal information processor, but it also requires the personal information processor to publicize the scope, purpose, and rules of processing personal information in a clear, understandable, and reasonable manner, and to accept external supervision.

IV. Principle of Quality

54. Article 8 of the "Personal Information Protection Law" stipulates that "the processing of personal information should ensure the quality of personal information and avoid adverse effects on personal rights and interests due to inaccurate or incomplete personal information." This article is a provision on the principle of quality. Before the promulgation of the "Personal Information Protection Law," some Chinese laws and regulations also required that the information processed by the information processor must be accurate and measures should be taken promptly when errors or omissions are found. Article 1037(1) of the "Civil Code" explicitly states, "Natural persons may check or copy their personal information with the information processor in accordance with the law; if errors are found in the information, they have the right to object and request necessary measures such as correction to be taken promptly." Article 23(1) of the "Credit Management Regulations" stipulates, "credit institutions should take reasonable measures to ensure the accuracy of the information they provide." Ensuring the quality of personal information is an important matter in the process of personal information processing because any falsehood, error, or distortion of the content of personal information can more or less affect the shaping of an individual's social image, causing the individual's development in society to deviate from their expectations.[26]

26. 最高人民法院民法典贯彻实施工作领导小组主编：《中华人民共和国民法典人格权编理解与适用》，人民法院出版社2020年版，第391页。Edited by the Leading Group for the Implementation of the Civil Code of the Supreme People's Court: "Interpretation and Application of the Personality Rights Section of the Civil Code of the People's Republic of China," (People's Court Press 2020 edition), p. 391.

The quality issues of personal information include two aspects: inaccurate personal information and incomplete personal information. "Inaccuracy" may mean that personal information is incorrect or outdated, and "incompleteness" includes the omission of some personal information or the newly generated personal information not being included.

V. Principle of Accountability and Security

55. In China's personal information protection legislation, the "accountability system" is adopted for personal information processing activities. Article 9 of the "Personal Information Protection Law" stipulates that "personal information processors should be responsible for their personal information processing activities and take necessary measures to ensure the security of the personal information they process." As the "Personal Information Protection Law" uniformly uses the term "processor," the processor is the primary responsible entity for personal information processing activities. On one hand, the processor determines the personal information and personal information processing activities, which generates a kind of "private power" and has control. Based on control theory, they naturally need to be responsible for their processing activities. On the other hand, according to the principle of compensation, where the benefits lie, the risks lie. Therefore, considering that personal information processors are generally the decision-makers, controllers, and beneficiaries of personal information processing activities, it is generally stipulated that personal information processors should be responsible for processing activities. And this responsibility includes both public law responsibilities and private law responsibilities. As far as public law responsibilities are concerned, the "Personal Information Protection Law" clearly sets out a series of obligations for personal information processors, and the fulfillment of these obligations is guaranteed by administrative responsibilities and even criminal responsibilities. In terms of private law responsibilities, Article 2 of the "Personal Information Protection Law," which stipulates that "the personal information of natural persons is protected by law," together with Article 9, constitutes the basis of the right to request for the protection of personal information rights and interests under civil law.

§2. The Legality Basis of Personal Information Processing

56. Objectively speaking, the act of processing personal information in itself constitutes an intrusion or impact on the personal information rights and interests of natural persons. This implies that, without a legal basis or legitimate reason, such processing activities can be considered illegal. Article 111, paragraph 2 of the "Civil Code" clearly states that "any organization or individual who needs to obtain personal information from others should do so in accordance with the law and ensure information security," while Article 44 of the "Cybersecurity Law" stipulates from the opposite perspective that " individuals or organizations must not steal or use other illegal methods to obtain personal information, and must not unlawfully sell or unlawfully provide others with personal information." Here, "obtaining in accordance with the law" means acquiring personal information based on a legitimate reason, "obtaining by illegal methods" signifies the lack of a legitimate reason to acquire personal information, and "unlawfully selling" or "unlawfully providing" refers to the sale or provision of obtained personal information to others without a legitimate reason. Article 13 of the "Personal Information Protection Law" concretizes the legitimate reasons and stipulates that "personal information processors may only process personal information under one of the following circumstances: (1) with the consent of the individual; (2) as necessary for the conclusion or performance of a contract to which the individual is a party, or as necessary for the implementation of human resources management in accordance with legally formulated labor rules and regulations and legally signed collective contracts; (3) as necessary for the performance of statutory duties or obligations; (4) as necessary to respond to public health emergencies or protect individuals' life, health, and property safety under emergency circumstances; (5) to carry out news reporting, public opinion-based supervision, and other activities in the public interest, and process personal information within a reasonable scope; (6) to process personal information within a reasonable scope in accordance with this law, that the individual has made public or that has been legally made public by others; (7) other circumstances stipulated by laws and administrative regulations".

57. In general, the legitimate reasons for processing personal information fall into two major categories: one is to obtain the individual's consent, that is, the legality of personal information processing activities comes from the valid consent of the information subject; the other is statutory reasons, that is, items 2 to 7 as stipulated in Article 13. When the conditions or reasons stipulated by laws and administrative regulations are met, the processor can carry out personal information processing activities without obtaining the individual's consent. Article 13 factually serves as a cornerstone within the entire Personal Information Protection Law, since the statute's primary objective is to regulate personal information processing activities, and this Article provides the benchmark for evaluating the legality of actions carried out by personal information processors. This implies that only if a personal information processing activity complies with one of the legal bases stipulated in Article 13, can it be further discussed whether it complies with the protection of personal information rights and interests. Among these, "with the consent of the individual" serves as the primary scenario allowing the processing of an individual's personal information. This underscores the pivotal role of informed consent within the framework of personal information processing regulations. The recognition of an individual's rights to their own information implies a limitation on the freedom of others' actions. That is, any action by an organization or individual to process personal information without the consent of the individual, when there are no other lawful reasons, constitutes an illegal act infringing on personal information rights. In addition to "with the consent of the individual," there are six other major categories of situations, such as "as necessary for the performance of statutory duties or obligations," where personal information can be legally processed. This implies that informing and obtaining individual consent is not the only legal basis for personal information processing, thus significantly expanding the scope of the legal basis for such processing. This is because the degree of protection of personal information cannot be as high as that of the right to life and the right to health, and the use of personal information is indispensable in modern society. Otherwise, the development of Internet technology and the digital economy would be impossible, and the ability of social governance and national governance would not be improved. Therefore, there are more restrictions on personal information rights. The six situations stipulated in Article 13 of the "Personal Information Protection Law," where personal information can be processed without obtaining the individual's consent, are a reflection of such restrictions.

§3. Special Types of Personal Information

I. Sensitive Personal Information

58. Although laws and regulations such as the "Civil Code" and "Cybersecurity Law" define the meaning of personal information, they do not distinguish between sensitive and non-sensitive personal information. Article 14 of the "Regulations on the Management of the Credit Reporting Industry" stipulates that "credit reporting agencies are prohibited from collecting personal information such as religious beliefs, genes, fingerprints, blood type, diseases and medical history, as well as other personal information that laws and administrative regulations prohibit from being collected." In reality, these are examples of sensitive personal information. The "Personal Information Protection Law," for the first time, legally adopts a classification of sensitive personal information and non-sensitive personal information. Regarding sensitive personal information, more stringent rules have been established. Article 28, paragraph 1, adopts a combination of generalization and enumeration, defining sensitive personal information as "personal information that, if leaked or illegally used, can easily infringe upon a natural person's dignity, or endanger their personal and property safety. This includes information on biometric identification, religious beliefs, specific identity, medical health, financial accounts, and personal whereabouts among others, as well as personal information of minors under fourteen years old."

59. As can be seen, Chinese legislation has focused on the most essential characteristic of sensitive personal information, that is, "sensitivity," meaning "if leaked or illegally used, it can easily infringe upon a natural person's dignity, or endanger their personal and property safety." The term "sensitivity" here refers to the likelihood of causing harm or damage. The consequences of this infringement or harm include two categories: One is the violation of personal dignity. Both Article 38 of the Constitution and Article 109 of the Civil Code stipulate that the personal freedom and dignity of Chinese citizens shall not be violated. The leakage or illegal use of sensitive personal information can easily lead to the violation of an individual's personal dignity. For example, if personal information such as one's ethnicity, race, illness, or sexual orientation is leaked or illegally used, it may lead to discrimination and unfair treatment. The other category involves endangerment to an individual's personal and property safety, that is, the infringement or risk of infringement on an individual's personal rights such as the right to life, body, and health, or on an individual's property rights.

60. Unlike non-sensitive personal information, processing sensitive personal information requires three prerequisites. According to Article 28, paragraph 2 of the "Personal Information Protection Law," "personal information processors may not process sensitive personal information unless there are specific purposes and sufficient necessity, and strict protection measures are taken." First, there must be a specific purpose. When dealing with sensitive personal information, a clear and reasonable purpose alone is not enough; it must also be a "specific purpose." Second, whether the processing purpose is specific should be judged in conjunction with the processing activities, such as providing services or products, fulfilling statutory duties or obligations, responding to public health emergencies, or maintaining public interest. Third, there must be sufficient necessity. The processing of sensitive personal information puts a strong emphasis on the protection of personal information rights and interest, requiring that collecting sensitive personal information is necessary to achieve a specific processing purpose. In other words, if the specific processing purpose can be achieved without collecting sensitive personal information, it should not be collected, and further processing activities should not be carried out. Fourth, strict protection measures should be taken. This is primarily reflected in the provisions of Chapter 5 of the "Personal Information Protection Law," which pertain to the obligations of personal information processors.

61. Processing sensitive personal information should be done with the individual's separate consent. Separate consent means that, in addition to adhering to the provisions of Article 14, paragraph 1 of the "Personal Information Protection Law," the personal information processor must specifically obtain consent from the individual regarding the processing of sensitive personal information, and such consent must be voluntary and explicit, made on the basis of being fully informed. In Chinese legislation, the processor cannot mix the processing of sensitive personal information with non-sensitive personal information and obtain the individual's consent in a lump sum manner. The processor must specifically inform and obtain consent for the processing of sensitive personal information, which is what we call separate consent with Chinese characteristics.

62. The personal information of minors under the age of 14 has also been legislatively defined as sensitive personal information. In order to process their information, consent should be obtained from the minor's parents or other guardians. This is because valid personal consent requires the consenting individual to have the ability to give consent, which is different from the capacity for civil conduct. The ability to consent refers to a natural person's understanding of the nature, extent, and possible consequences of their independent decision-making. Given the cognitive and comprehension limitations of minors, and the legal principle of "what's most beneficial for minors," the "Personal Information Protection Law" provides special protection for them. That is, in order to process their personal information, consent must be obtained from their parents or other guardians. In addition, Article 31, paragraph 2 of the "Personal Information Protection Law" stipulates that "when personal information processors process the personal information of minors under the age of fourteen, they should formulate specific rules for such processing." This implies that the processor should have at least two sets of personal information processing rules. One is specifically formulated for the processing of personal information of minors under the age of 14, applicable only in such cases. The other can be generally applicable to all other personal information processing. This serves to remind the processor of the heavier obligations and responsibilities they bear when handling children's personal information, so as to prevent any infringement on children's rights and interests.

II. Personal Information of the Deceased

63. Chinese law has always protected the personality rights and interests of the deceased. For example, Article 994 of the Civil Code states, "If the name, likeness, reputation, honor, privacy, remains, or the like of the deceased is harmed, the spouse, children, and parents of the deceased have the right to request the perpetrator to bear civil liability in accordance with law. If the deceased has no spouse or children, and the parents are deceased, other close relatives have the right to request the perpetrator to bear civil liability in accordance with law." Regarding the personal information of the deceased, if the deceased's close relatives are unrestrictedly granted the right to exercise the rights the deceased had during their lifetime in the handling of personal information, it could go against the wishes of the deceased and infringe on the privacy rights of third parties. Therefore, Article 49 of the "Personal Information Protection Law" stipulates, "where a natural person dies, his or her close relatives, for their own legal and legitimate interests, can exercise the rights to consult, duplicate, correct, delete the relevant personal information of the deceased, among others, unless the deceased had made other arrangements before his or her death." This suggests that the "Personal Information Protection Law" is designed to safeguard the personal information of living individuals, not those of the deceased. The rationale behind allowing the close relatives of the deceased to exercise these rights is to protect the legal and legitimate interests of these close relatives themselves, rather than safeguarding the interests of others. However, respecting the legal and valid wishes of the deceased is an important principle in civil law activities. Therefore, if the deceased had made "arrangements" for their personal information while they were alive, these arrangements should be carried out in accordance with their wishes.

Part IV. Rights of the Subject of Personal Information

64. Based on the provisions of the "Cybersecurity Law" and the "Civil Code," Chapter 4 of the "Personal Information Protection Law" methodically outlines the array of rights individuals possess during personal information processing activities. These rights against personal information processors encompass the right to know, right to decide, right to consult and duplicate, right to data portability, right to rectification, right to erasure, and right to explanations.

§1. Right to Know, Right to Decide

65. Article 44 of the "Personal Information Protection Law" states: "An individual has the right to know and decide about the processing of his or her personal information, and has the right to restrict or refuse others from processing his or her personal information, except as otherwise provided by laws and administrative regulations." This article establishes the right to know and decide what the subject of personal information enjoys. These rights serve as the fundamental and generalized rights of individuals in personal information processing activities.

66. The right to know refers to the right of an individual to be informed about the relevant circumstances in the processing of his or her personal information. An individual has the right to know who is processing which of their personal information, for what purpose, and in what way. The right to know embodies the principle of openness and transparency, corresponding to the disclosure obligations of the processors stipulated in Articles 17, 23, and 30 of the "Personal Information Protection Law." The right to know includes being informed before personal information is processed, demanding that the personal information processor discloses their processing rules, as well as rights to consult and duplicate, and rights to explanations of the rules.

67. The right to decide refers to an individual's right to determine who processes their personal information, for what purpose, in what manner, and within what scope, unless otherwise stipulated by laws or administrative regulations. In general, the right to decide includes consenting to others processing their personal information, as well as restricting or refusing others from processing their personal information. Specifically, it includes: (1) any processor must, in principle, inform the individual and obtain their consent before processing personal information. The processor may not exceed the agreed-upon purpose, method, or type of personal information processed. If changes are needed, the processor must reinform the individual and obtain their renewed consent (Article 14); (2) if the processor is to provide personal information to others, to provide personal information abroad, to publicly disclose the personal information they process, to process sensitive personal information, or to use the collected personal images or identification information for purposes other than maintaining public safety, they must all obtain separate consent from the individual; (3) an individual has the right to withdraw their consent at any time (Article 15); (4) an individual has the right to data portability, the right to rectification, and the right to erasure; (5) an individual has the right to refuse the processing of public information and the right to refuse automated decision-making.

68. The right to know and the right to decide are not absolute rights. The restrictions on the right to know are mainly reflected in Article 18, paragraph 1, which states that processors are permitted not to notify the individual of personal information processing if laws and administrative regulations provide that such processing shall be kept confidential or notification is necessary. The limitations on the right to make decisions manifest in situations specified in Article 13, where consent isn't required, and in restrictions on the overseas transfer of personal data, as outlined in Article 40.

§2. Right to Consult and Duplicate

69. Article 45, paragraphs 1 and 2 of the "Personal Information Protection Law" stipulates the right to consult and duplicate, "Individuals have the right to consult and duplicate their personal information from personal information processors, except for circumstances stipulated in the first paragraph of Article 18 and Article 35 of this law." Article 1037, paragraph 1 of the "Civil Code" stipulates, "Natural persons can consult or duplicate their personal information from information processors in accordance with law." The right to consult and duplicate is the implementation of the principle of openness and transparency stipulated in Article 7 of the "Personal Information Protection Law," and it is also an important part of the right to know stated in Article 44 of this law. The right to consult and duplicate is also the basic right for subsequent rights such as the right to data portability, right to rectification, and right to erasure. If an individual cannot access and copy their personal information, the personal information processing activity does not comply with the principle of openness and transparency, and the individual cannot exercise the rights such as the rights to data portability, correction, and deletion.

70. The subject of the right to consult and duplicate is the natural person whose personal information is being processed. Under Article 49 of the "Personal Information Protection Law," if the natural person has passed away, his or her close relatives can exercise such right, unless the deceased had made different arrangements while still alive. Chinese legislation does not specify the detailed procedures for exercising the right to consult and duplicate. However, when exercising this right, individuals should prove their real identity in an appropriate manner. Under specific circumstances, individuals are not allowed to exercise the right to consult and duplicate: first, in scenarios where laws and administrative regulations state that the information must remain confidential or doesn't need to be disclosed; second, when such disclosure could potentially interfere with a state agency's performance of its legal responsibilities.

71. Article 45, paragraph 2 of the "Personal Information Protection Law" stipulates, "When an individual requests to consult or duplicate his or her personal information, the personal information processor should provide it promptly." Furthermore, Article 23 of the "Regulations on Network Data Security Management (Draft for Soliciting Opinions)" stipulates that upon receiving an individual's application to copy his or her own personal information, it should be processed and responded to within fifteen working days.

§3. Right to Data Portability

72. The right to data portability refers to the right of an individual, under certain conditions, to request the transfer of their personal information, processed by a personal information processor, to another personal information processor. Article 45, paragraph 3 of the "Personal Information Protection Law" stipulates, "When an individual requests the transfer of personal information to his or her designated personal information processor, and it complies with the conditions stipulated by the national cyberspace authority, the personal information processor should provide the channels for the transfer." This clause is considered to constitute the right to data portability or the right to transfer personal information. This right has two significant implications: first, it enhances an individual's control over their personal information; second, it reduces potential data monopolies that large Internet companies could create by leveraging their market advantage, mitigating the "lock-in effect" and improving market competition.

73. The "Personal Information Protection Law" does not provide specific requirements for exercising the right to data portability, instead authorizing the national cyberspace authority to establish the conditions for exercising this right. In this regard, Article 24 of the "Regulations on Network Data Security Management (Draft for Soliciting Opinions)" makes a preliminary stipulation on the conditions for exercising the right to data portability: "Data processors should provide a transfer service for another data processor designated by the individual to access and obtain their personal information, if the request for data transfer meets the following conditions: (1) The personal information requested for transfer is collected based on consent or is necessary for concluding or fulfilling a contract; (2) The personal information requested for transfer is the requester's own information or someone else's information that the requester has legally obtained and does not violate the other person's will; (3) The legal identity of the requester can be verified. If the data processor finds that the other data processor receiving the personal information has a risk of illegally processing personal information, they should provide reasonable risk warnings for the request. If the number of requests to transfer personal information significantly exceeds a reasonable range, the data processor can charge a reasonable fee."

§4. RIGHT TO RECTIFICATION

74. Article 46, paragraph 1 of the "Personal Information Protection Law" stipulates: "If an individual finds that his or her personal information is inaccurate or incomplete, he or she has the right to request the personal information processor to correct or supplement it." This provision is about the right to rectification, which means that individuals have the right to request the personal information processor to correct and supplement inaccurate or incomplete personal information. Inaccurate personal information refers to cases where the personal information processed by the processor does not match the actual personal information. Incomplete personal information refers to situations where there are omissions and missing information in the personal information. The right to rectification is a requirement of the principle of quality for personal information protection. Especially when it involves significant personal rights and interests, the right to rectification becomes particularly important. Similarly, Article 43 of the "Cybersecurity Law" states that if an individual finds errors in their personal information collected and stored by network operators, they have the right to request corrections from the network operators. Also, Article 1037, paragraph 1 of the "Civil Code" provides that if a natural person finds an error in the information, they have the right to raise objections and request timely correction and other necessary measures.

75. Article 46, paragraph 2 of the "Personal Information Protection Law" stipulates: "When an individual requests correction or supplementation of their personal information, the personal information processor should verify their personal information, and correct or supplement it in a timely manner." Based on this clause, the personal information processor should verify the applicant's personal information to determine whether there are uncertainties or inaccuracies. When necessary, the processor can ask the applicant to provide relevant materials. If indeed the applicant's personal information is uncertain or inaccurate, the personal information processor should correct or supplement it in a timely manner. If there is no such situation, the processor should explain the reasons for refusal to the applicant. "Timely" means that the personal information processor should not delay. In practice, the time required for the processor to make corrections or supplements should be determined based on factors such as the difficulty of making the correction or supplement.

§5. RIGHT TO ERASURE

76. The right to erasure refers to the individual's right to request the information processor to delete their personal information in the event of a lawful or mutually agreed-upon circumstance. According to Article 43 of the "Cybersecurity Law," individuals have the right to request the deletion of their personal information by network operators if they find that the operators have violated laws, administrative regulations, or agreements in the collection and use of their personal information. Also, Article 1037, paragraph 2 of the "Civil Code" stipulates that if natural persons find that an information processor has violated laws, administrative regulations, or agreements in handling their personal information, they have the right to request the information processor to delete it promptly.

77. Based on the aforementioned regulations, the "Personal Information Protection Law" further refines the provisions concerning the right to erasure. Article 47 stipulates that the personal information processor should actively delete personal information under five scenarios. If the personal information processor does not delete it, the individual has the right to request deletion. The five scenarios include: (1) The processing purpose has been achieved, cannot be achieved, or is no longer necessary to achieve the processing purpose. This is a specific manifestation of the principle of purpose limitation in Article 6 of the "Personal Information Protection Law." (2) The personal information processor stops providing products or services, or the retention period has expired. This specifically includes scenarios where the personal information processor has fulfilled the contract established with the individual, both parties have agreed to terminate the contract, or the personal information processor has ceased to exist or gone bankrupt, and therefore can no longer provide products or services. Whether the legally mandated retention period or the agreed retention period has expired, the personal information processor should actively delete the personal information. (3) The individual withdraws consent. Article 15, paragraph 1 of the "Personal Information Protection Law" stipulates that if the processing of personal information is based on the individual's consent, the individual has the right to withdraw this consent. When the individual withdraws consent, the personal information processor should proactively, or upon the individual's request, delete their personal information. (4) The personal information processor processes personal information in violation of laws, administrative regulations, or agreements. That is, if the processor's handling of personal information is unlawful or violates an agreement, the individual has the right to request deletion. (5) Other circumstances stipulated by laws and administrative regulations. When the individual requests the processor to delete their information, he or she should provide proof that there are circumstances warranting deletion.

78. Article 47 of the "Personal Information Protection Law" also clarifies the limitations on the exercise of the right to deletion, that is, scenarios where the individual cannot exercise the right to delete. This involves two scenarios: (1) From a legal perspective, the right to deletion is not permissible when the retention period set forth by laws and administrative regulations has not yet been reached. The legislation takes into account that, in some cases, personal information also includes public interests, and laws and administrative regulations have stipulated corresponding retention periods for personal information. For example, Article 137 of the "Securities Law" stipulates that the retention period for customer information should not be less than twenty years; Article 24 of the "Electronic Signature Law" stipulates that the retention period for authentication information should be at least five years after the electronic signature certificate has expired. (2) On a practical level, the deletion of personal information may not be feasible since it is technically difficult to achieve. With the widespread application of information technology, there are technical situations where it is impossible to completely delete personal information, and legislation has left room for this. "It is technically difficult to achieve" should be understood as the current technology being incapable of deleting the information, or that it would require unreasonable costs to delete the information under the current technology. However, in the aforementioned situations where the individual cannot exercise the right to deletion, the personal information processor should properly store the above-mentioned information, take corresponding security measures, and not use the personal information for further processing; all other processing activities should cease.

§6. Right to Explanation

79. Article 48 of the "Personal Information Protection Law" stipulates that individuals have the right to request that personal information processors explain the rules for processing their personal information. At present, personal information processing rules often suffer from issues like being overly verbose, hard to comprehend, and having vague language. These issues could lead to differing understandings of these rules among individuals, which can impact the exercise of an individual's rights to be informed and make decisions. Therefore, it is necessary to stipulate the right to explanation of personal information processing rules. Personal information processing rules are usually stipulated in privacy policies or contract terms, unilaterally established by the personal information processor. The right to an explanation thus aligns with the principles of the "Civil Code" regarding the provisions on standard contract terms. Specifically, Article 496, paragraph 2 of the "Civil Code" stipulates that when a contract is formed using standard terms, the party providing the standard terms should determine the rights and obligations between the parties according to the principle of fairness. They should also reasonably alert the other party to clauses that are of significant interest to them, such as those that exempt or mitigate their liabilities, and explain these clauses as per the other party's request. If the party providing the standard terms fails to fulfill their obligation to alert or explain, causing the other party not to notice or understand the clauses that have significant interests related to them, the other party can claim that these clauses do not form part of the contract. When it comes to exercising the right to explanation, it is the responsibility of the personal information processor to provide easy and accessible methods and avenues for individuals to request explanations about the rules governing the processing of their personal information. After receiving a request from individuals, they should explain their personal information processing rules in plain and understandable language within a reasonable time.

80. The right to explanatory interpretation should be distinguished from the right to explanation in automated decision-making. The right to explanatory interpretation mainly pertains to the explanation of rules for processing personal information, while the right to explanation in automated decision-making carries a different meaning. Article 24, paragraph 3 of the "Personal Information Protection Law" stipulates, "When a decision that significantly impacts an individual's rights and interests is made through automated decision-making, the individual has the right to request an explanation from the personal information processor." This provision constitutes the right to algorithmic explanation in automated decision-making, which is a manifestation of the individual's right to be informed, and also forms the basis for the individual's exercise of decision-making rights. To a certain extent, the right to algorithmic explanation rectifies the lack of due process protection in automated decision-making, safeguarding an individual's right to be informed and to make decisions about automated decisions. The premise for applying this provision is that the decision "has a significant impact on an individual's rights and interests through automated decision-making." The personal information processor should assess such impacts. Article 55, paragraph 2 of the "Personal Information Protection Law" stipulates that when using personal information for automated processing, the personal information processor has the obligation to conduct a prior assessment of the impact on personal information protection, and to record the processing situation.

§7. Right to Refuse

81. Article 44 of the "Personal Information Protection Law" stipulates the right to decision-making, which includes the content of restricting or refusing others to process their personal information.In addition to the right to consent, the act of restricting or refusing the processing of personal information by the processor also reflects the individual's decision-making rights. Article 24, paragraphs 2 and 3 of the "Personal Information Protection Law" respectively stipulate the right to refuse personalized recommendations based on automated decision-making, and the right to refuse automated decision-making.

82. Article 24, paragraph 2 of the "Personal Information Protection Law" stipulates, "When pushing information or conducting commercial marketing to an individual through automated decision-making, options that are not targeted at the individual's characteristics should be provided at the same time, or a convenient way for the individual to refuse should be provided." Article 18, paragraph 1 of the "E-commerce Law" states, "When an e-commerce operator provides search results of goods or services based on the consumer's interests, hobbies, consumption habits, and other characteristics, it should concurrently provide options that do not target the consumer's personal characteristics to ensure the respect and equal protection of the consumer's legitimate rights and interests." The stipulation in the "Personal Information Protection Law" complements the content of Article 18, paragraph 1 of the "E-commerce Law." This provision takes into account that during the automated decision-making process, decisions may be made based on inaccurate or incomplete information, which may infringe upon individuals' personal information rights and interests. In the main application scenarios of automated decision-making, such as information push and commercial marketing, the Personal

Information Protection Law provides two choices for personal information processors: First, the processors could present both personalized (based on individual characteristics) and non-personalized information on their service page, thereby allowing individuals to discern and make their own choices. Second, the processors could provide the option for individuals to reject targeted services based on their characteristics. The applicability of this right of refusal is evident in contexts such as personalized recommendations or user profiling in automated decision-making. It's imperative for information processors to offer individuals an easy-to-use mechanism to exercise their right to refuse.

83. Article 24, paragraph 3 of the "Personal Information Protection Law" stipulates that when decisions that significantly impact an individual's rights and interests are made through automated decision-making methods, the individual has the right to request an explanation from the personal information processor, and has the right to refuse the personal information processor to make decisions solely through automated decision-making methods. This provision stipulates the right to refuse automated decision-making. It grants individuals the right to request human intervention in decisions made through automated methods that significantly impact personal rights and interests. The individual can require the personal information processor to manually intervene and review whether the automated decision was made fairly and justly, and they can also request corrections of incorrect or inappropriate decision outcomes. Unlike the right to withdraw consent at will as stipulated in Article 16 of the "Personal Information Protection Law," the exercise of the right to refuse automated decision-making must meet certain conditions. It primarily includes two elements: first, it must be a decision made solely through automated decision-making methods. As long as no one has decision-making power during the decision-making process and cannot influence the content of the decision, the decision can be considered made solely through automated decision-making, regardless of whether the individual participated in the decision-making process or not. In addition, the right to refuse automated decision-making is not limited to the processing of personal information based on consent. Any decision made solely through automated decision-making methods can be subject to this right. Second, it must have a significant impact on the individual's rights and interests. Individual rights and interests encompass any rights related to the individual, not limited to those specified in the "Personal Information Protection Law." The so-called "significant impact" not only includes negative effects but also positive ones. It generally refers to changes in the individual's legal rights, obligations, and responsibilities, or changes in the individual's economic or social status. However, whether these changes significantly affect the individual needs to be judged on a case-by-case basis. Additionally, an individual cannot subjectively assume that automated decision-making has a significant impact on their rights and interests. They also bear the corresponding burden of proof.

§8. OTHER RIGHTS

84. Article 50, paragraph 1 of the "Personal Information Protection Law" stipulates that, "Personal information processors should establish a convenient mechanism for accepting and handling applications for individuals to exercise their rights. If they refuse a request from an individual to exercise their rights, they must provide a reason." This provision stipulates that personal information processors should establish corresponding mechanisms to protect individuals' exercise of rights, as well as judicial remedies after the refusal of individuals' exercise of rights. As stipulated in Chapter 4 of the "Personal Information Protection Law," these rights include the right to know, right to decide, right to consult and duplicate, right to data portability, right to rectification, right to erasure, right to explanation, right to refuse, etc. The obligation subjects of the above rights are personal information processors. They need to fulfill their corresponding obligations in order to realize the rights of individuals.

85. When personal information processors respond to individuals' requests to exercise their rights, they should meet the following requirements. First, they should establish an application acceptance mechanism, which specifically includes the method of submitting applications, the institutions or individuals accepting applications, the materials that should be submitted when applying, feedback on accepting applications, and so forth. Second, they should establish an application handling mechanism, including the institutions or personnel handling applications after acceptance, the handling process, and feedback on the handling results. Third, the application acceptance and handling mechanisms of personal information processors should be convenient and should not set up unreasonable obstacles. Fourth, personal information processors should provide reasons when they refuse a request from an individual to exercise their rights.

86. Article 50, paragraph 2 of the "Personal Information Protection Law" stipulates, "If a personal information processor refuses a request from an individual to exercise their rights, the individual may file a lawsuit in a People's Court according to the law." When an individual's rights in personal information processing activities cannot be exercised, that is, when a request to exercise their rights is refused by a personal information processor, the individual has the right to file a lawsuit in the People's Court. An individual's inability to exercise their rights can occur both when a personal information processor declines the request through written or verbal communication and when the processor does not respond to the individual's request within a reasonable period.

87. The rights of individuals as data subjects, as outlined from Article 44 onward in the "Personal Information Protection Law," complement and perfect the relevant provisions in the "Cybersecurity Law" and the "Civil Code." They detail the provisions on the rights to inquiry, duplication, rectification, and erasure, and the newly added right to data portability is also of significant importance. Personal information intrinsically holds value similar to property, and it is essentially a type of personality rights including property interests.[27] Individuals' rights in personal information activities are instrumental or remedial in nature.[28] This means that these rights can be enjoyed by individuals only in the context of personal information processing activities. However, such rights are not absolute, and they can be limited by laws and regulations.[29]

27. 彭诚信：《论个人信息的双重法律属性》，载《清华法学》2021年第6期。Peng Chengxin, "On the Dual Legal Attributes of Personal Information," in "Tsinghua Law Review," 6 (2021).
28. 程啸：《个人信息保护法理解与适用》，中国法制出版社2021年版，第327页。Cheng Xiao, "Understanding and Application of the Personal Information Protection Law," (China Legal System Publishing House 2021 edition), p. 327.
29. 杨合庆主编：《个人信息保护法释义》，法律出版社2022年版，第113页。Yang Heqing (Editor-in-chief), "Interpretation of the Personal Information Protection Law," (Legal Publishing House 2022 edition), p. 113.

Part V. Obligations of Personal Information Processors

88. Even before the advent of the digital society, personal information existed, and the law provided corresponding protection based on the rights and interests carried by the information.

89. For instance, laws protect personal information such as name, portrait, and privacy through mechanisms like the right to name, right to likeness, and right to privacy, prohibiting others from illegal processing. However, with the advent of the digital society, the application of intelligent algorithms has led to an increasingly diverse range of personal information types. The entities involved in processing personal information have become more diverse, and the processing activities themselves have become more complex. As a result, a complex web of legal relationships has emerged. It is thus necessary to specify the obligations of personal information processors, linking them with the rights framework in personal information protection. This primarily includes the obligations to adopt preliminary prevention measures, to provide timely remedies after the accident, and to comply with specific regulations for special contexts and entities.

§1. Processors' Preliminary Prevention Obligation

90. The preliminary prevention obligations of personal information processors mainly involve two aspects, internal and external. From an external perspective, the "Personal Information Protection Law" distinguishes different stages of personal information processing, different types of personal information, and different personal information processors, clarifying the preventive obligations of personal information processors, such as notifying and obtaining the consent of the subject of the personal information. From an internal perspective, the "Personal Information Protection Law" requires personal information processors to establish management systems and operational procedures that align with their industry characteristics when processing personal information. This includes implementing tiered protections for personal information and adopting technical safety defenses like encryption and de-identification throughout the entire lifecycle of the personal information. The law also stipulates a preliminary impact assessment system for personal information protection, to eliminate potential risks at the earliest stage, thus aligning with the principle of risk minimization.

91. Article 17 stipulates the general notification rules for personal information processors. The notification and consent rule is a core rule in personal information protection norms. It requires that the processing of personal information must be preceded by sufficient prior notification, and the consent of the subject of personal information must be obtained. The "Personal Information Protection Law" stipulates the obligation of notification, emphasizing not only the importance of notification but also addressing situations where consent rules cannot be applied. In other words, the notification rules also apply in situations where personal consent is not required, in order to ensure the right to information of the data subject. Furthermore, this provision also specifies the content, methods, and standards of notification. First, the notification should include the identity or name of the personal information processor, contact information, the purpose, method, content, and retention period of the processing, as well as the procedures for individuals to exercise their rights. Second, the notification should be provided to the data subject in a "prominent and easily understandable" manner, in order to avoid situations where technical obscurity and difficulty hinder the data subject's awareness of the scenarios, purposes, methods, and scope of information processing. Third, the content of the notification should adhere to the standards of "truthfulness, accuracy, and completeness," ensuring that the data subject's right to be informed is fully realized. This can strengthen the transparency of personal information processing and provide comprehensive and dynamic protection of the rights and interests of the data subject. Fourthly, the "Personal Information Protection Law" imposes special notification obligations for certain specific personal information processing activities. For example, Article 22 specifies the matters that should be notified to the data subject when transferring personal information through merger, separation, dissolution, and other means. Article 23 stipulates the matters that should be notified to the data subject when providing personal information to other personal information processors, as well as situations requiring separate consent. Article 30 stipulates the special notification matters when processing sensitive personal information. Article 39 specifies the matters that should be notified when providing personal information across borders. These provisions intend to ensure that the data subject is fully informed before personal information processing takes place and can make a voluntary and explicit choice regarding consent.

92. Article 51 of the "Personal Information Protection Law" stipulates that personal information processors have a duty of care throughout the entire lifecycle of processing personal information. They should adopt corresponding security management measures based on the purpose, method, type of personal information processed, the impact on individual rights and interests, and potential risks to ensure the legality and security of personal information processing. First of all, personal information processors should formulate internal management systems and operating procedures. Internal management systems refer to rules established by the processor regarding management structure, personnel allocation, and responsibilities, while operating procedures refer to procedural regulations that should be adhered to when operating related equipment or handling business.[30] This provision continues the regulation of Article 21 of the Cybersecurity Law on the system of cybersecurity hierarchical protection. In order to fully utilize the preventive function of personal information security measures, the Personal Information Protection Law requires personal information processors to cover all aspects of personal information processing in their internal management and operating procedures. Second, personal information processors should manage personal information by classification, that is, adopting differentiated protection measures according to different categories of personal information. Processing different personal information leads to different security risks. For example, the harm caused by the infringement of sensitive personal information is greater than that of general personal information. Third, personal information processors should adopt such security technology measures as encryption and de-identification to ensure the compliance of personal information processing with laws and administrative regulations and effectively prevent such unauthorized access as the leakage, theft, alteration, or deletion of personal information. Finally, it is important to appropriately set operational permissions for personal information processing and regularly provide security education and training for employees. This will help to establish an internal management mechanism that features coordinated division of labor, mutual checks and supervision.

93. Within the system of Personal Information Protection Impact Assessment, Article 55 of the "Personal Information Protection Law" stipulates the obligation for conducting and documenting such assessments, while Article 56 provides detailed provisions on the content of these assessments. First, Article 55 requires that personal information processors, when handling personal information under specific circumstances, should assess the impact on personal information protection beforehand and document the processing activities. This primarily involves carrying out an initial evaluation and documentation for certain high-risk personal information processing activities. These steps are essential in securing the safety and legality of personal information handling procedures. The main applicable circumstances include processing sensitive personal information; using personal information for automated decision-making; outsourcing personal information processing; providing personal information to other processors, or disclosing personal information to the public; providing personal information overseas, and other personal information processing activities that have a significant impact on personal rights and interests. Second, since the personal information protection impact assessment targets processing activities that pose a higher risk to personal rights and interests, the content of the assessment should comply with the principles of legality, legitimacy, and necessity. Article 56 of the "Personal Information Protection Law" provides specific provisions on the content of the personal information protection impact assessment, mainly including: (1) whether the processing purpose and method of personal information are legal, legitimate, and necessary; (2) the impact on personal rights

30. 参见龙卫球主编：《中华人民共和国个人信息保护法释义》，中国法制出版社2021年版，第232页。Long Weiqiu (Editor-in-chief), "Interpretation of the Personal Information Protection Law of the People's Republic of China," (China Legal System Publishing House 2021 edition), p. 232.

and interests and security risks; and (3) whether the security measures adopted are legal, effective, and commensurate with the level of risk. In addition, the risk assessment report and processing records for personal information protection should also be preserved for three years. This ensures that when a personal information security incident occurs, the facts of the case and the responsible person can be identified.

§2. Processors' Post-hoc Timely Remediation Obligation

94. When a personal information security incident occurs, how to provide relief to individuals and prevent the enlargement of damages to their rights and interests is an important goal of the personal information protection system. Article 42, paragraph 2 of China's "Cybersecurity Law" and Article 1038, paragraph 2 of the "Civil Code" both stipulate remedial measures and notification systems for personal information security incidents. Based on these provisions, Article 57 of the "Personal Information Protection Law" further refines the remedial measures and notification obligations of personal information processors. It clarifies the content of the notification and the circumstances in which the notification is not given. It also grants departments responsible for fulfilling personal information protection duties the power to compel personal information processors to notify individuals.

95. Personal information security incidents mainly refer to scenarios where there has been, or there's a likelihood of, personal information being leaked, altered, or lost. Once an incident occurs, the personal information processor should immediately take remedial measures, promptly ascertain the cause of such an incident, and take corresponding measures to minimize the damage. When taking remedial measures, processors need to consider such factors as the quantity, nature, and sensitivity of the personal information leaked, altered, or lost. The more personal information involved and the higher its sensitivity, the greater the risk to individuals' rights and interests, and the more serious the consequences of the damage. Also, after an incident occurs, processors are required to execute distinct notification responsibilities depending on the particular circumstances.

96. Moreover, the "Personal Information Protection Law" establishes a tripartite categorization for notifications that personal information processors are obligated to issue: obligatory notification, discretionary notification, and directive notification. In the event of a potential or actual personal information security incident, it is obligatory for the personal information processors to alert both the department tasked with personal information protection and the affected individuals. If the processor's preventative measures are likely to effectively avert any impending harm, the decision to notify the individual rests at their discretion. However, informing the designated personal information protection department remains a requisite. Should the department discern any residual risk to the individuals despite the preventive actions implemented by the processor, it retains the jurisdiction to mandate the processor to issue notifications to the concerned individuals. Finally, the essence of the notification encompasses crucial details such as the type of personal information implicated in the security incident, the root cause of the incident, and the potential harm that might ensue. This comprehensive approach ensures that the individual's right to be fully informed is respected and upheld.

§3. PROCESSORS' SUPPORTING MEASURES FOR SECURITY ASSURANCE

97. To ensure that personal information processors fulfill their security and compliance obligations and protect the security of personal information, the "Personal Information Protection Law" regulates personal information processing activities from both internal and external perspectives. Internally, Article 54 of the "Personal Information Protection Law" requires personal information processors to regularly fulfill compliance audit obligations, which is an inherent requirement of the legality principle of personal information processing behavior. Whether the internal management of personal information processors is lawful is an important prerequisite for data compliance. Regular compliance audits of personal information processing activities are crucial measures to avoid incurring legal responsibilities due to noncompliant processing behaviors.

98. Externally, imitating the data protection officer system in Germany and the European Union, Article 52 establishes the personal information protection officer system, aimed at supervising and managing the activities of personal information processors. The "Personal Information Protection Law" does not require all personal information processors to appoint a personal information protection officer but rather targets "personal information processors who handle personal information up to the quantity stipulated by the national cyberspace authority." In other words, whether to establish a personal information protection officer depends on the standard of the quantity of personal information processing determined by the national cyberspace authority. For example, the "Information Security Technology—Personal Information Security Specification" (GB/T35273-2020) stipulates that a dedicated personal information protection officer should be appointed if the following quantity standards are met, i.e., the main business involves personal information processing, the scale of employees exceeds 200, and the processor handles personal information of more than 1 million people or sensitive personal information of more than 100,000 people.

99. After appointing a personal information protection officer, the personal information processor should disclose the contact information of the officer in order to facilitate supervision by individuals and the exercise of their corresponding rights. Meanwhile, the processor also needs to report the name and contact information of the officer to the department responsible for personal information protection. The main duty of the personal information protection officer is to conduct continuous supervision and management of the personal information processor's processing activities. For example, he or she should coordinate personal information protection tasks and urge their implementation, publicize the methods for reporting complaints and implement them promptly, and conduct security audits of personal information processing activities.

100. It is worth noting that Article 21, Item 1 of the "Cybersecurity Law" requires network operators to formulate internal security management systems and operating procedures in accordance with the requirements of the cybersecurity level protection system and to appoint a cybersecurity person in charge. The "cybersecurity persons in charge" mentioned here is different from the "personal information protection officer." The cybersecurity person in charge must be appointed by network operators, and he or she must also fulfill the obligation of cybersecurity protection. There is no requirement for the amount of personal information in this case.

101. In addition, Article 53 of the "Personal Information Protection Law" also stipulates requirements for overseas personal information processors to establish specialized institutions or designate representatives. This clause only requires overseas personal information processors to establish specialized institutions or designate representatives in China to handle matters related to personal information protection. It does not require the establishment of personal information protection officers. Additionally, overseas personal information processors should report the names of relevant institutions or the names and contact information of designated representatives to the department responsible for personal information protection for supervision purposes.

§4. Obligations in Cases Involving Multiple Information Processors

102. Article 20 of the "Personal Information Protection Law" stipulates the scenarios involving the joint processing of personal information and joint liability for compensation of the processors. The Chinese legislation does not emulate the European Union in distinguishing between "controllers" and "processors," but uses the unified term "personal information processor," which covers all subjects involved in the processing of personal information. According to Article 20, paragraph 1: "When two or more personal information processors jointly determine the purpose and method of processing personal information, they should agree on their respective rights and obligations." It can be seen that the criterion for judging "joint processors" is jointly determining the purpose and method of processing personal information.[31] When joint processors violate the purpose and method of personal information processing, infringe on personal information rights and interests, and cause damage, they shall bear joint and several liabilities.

103. Article 21 of the "Personal Information Protection Law" stipulates the situations of entrusted processing, mainly referring to the situations where a personal information processor entrusts another person or organization to process personal information, establishing a relationship of entrustment between both parties. Under Article 55, paragraph 3 of this law, the personal information processor should carry

31. 参见程啸：《论个人信息共同处理者的民事责任》，载《法学家》2021年第6期，第24页。
Cheng Xiao, "On the Civil Liability of Co-Processors of Personal Information," in "Jurist," 6 (2021), p. 24.

out a prior assessment of personal information protection and keep records of the processing situation, thereby effectively reducing the potential risks caused by personal information processing. Based on this, the principal and the trustee should enter into an entrustment contract, stipulating essential terms such as the purpose, term, method of the entrusted processing, the type of personal information, protection measures, and the rights and obligations of both parties. The form of the contract can be in writing, verbal, or electronic. Also, the principal has the obligation to supervise the trustee's processing of personal information to ensure that the trustee processes it for the purpose stipulated in the contract, ensuring the security of personal information. The trustee should fulfill the obligation to process personal information in accordance with the contract stipulations or legal provisions and should not re-entrust it to others for processing without the consent of the principal. When the entrustment contract is invalid, revoked, or not in effect, the trustee should return the personal information to the principal or delete it and may not retain it. In addition, the trustee should also take necessary measures to ensure the security of personal information and assist the principal in fulfilling relevant compliance obligations.

104. Under Article 22 of the "Personal Information Protection Law," a personal information processor is allowed to transfer personal information when there is a change in its legal status. The reasons for such changes include mergers, divisions, declaration of bankruptcy, and dissolution. In such cases, the personal information processor should inform the individual of the name and contact information of the recipient. The recipient is then responsible for fulfilling the obligations of the personal information processor in accordance with the relevant laws or contractual agreements. Moreover, if the recipient changes the original purpose or method of processing personal information, except where the law specifies that obtaining personal consent is not required, it or he should fulfill the obligation of re-notification to the individual in advance and re-obtain their consent.

105. Article 23 of the "Personal Information Protection Law" stipulates the situations in which personal information is provided to other personal information processors. It is predicted that after the personal information is provided to another party, the recipient may process the personal information according to its own purposes and scope of processing. In this situation, the individual will effectively lose control over their personal information. Therefore, the "Personal Information Protection Law" establishes two mechanisms of separate consent and re-consent to regulate such situations. When a personal information processor provides personal information to another party, it or he must inform the individual of the recipient's name or identity, contact information, purpose of processing, method of processing, and type of personal information involved and obtain the individual's separate consent for such provision. The recipient is not allowed to change the purpose and method of processing without obtaining the individual's consent. If any changes are made, the recipient must re-obtain the individual's consent.

§5. The Gatekeeper Obligation of Large-Scale Processors

106. Article 58 of the "Personal Information Protection Law" provides detailed provisions on the duties of special personal information processors. Special personal information processors refer to those who provide significant Internet platform services, have a large user base, and engage in complex business operations. In simple terms, they refer to the operators of large Internet platforms, also known as the "gatekeepers" of the Internet ecosystem. The reason for establishing specific obligations for this particular entity is that gatekeepers control the technical and operational environment of Internet and mobile applications. They have strong technical and control capabilities and play a decisive role in technical settings and specific actions related to personal information protection.[32] Therefore, in addition to fulfilling general compliance obligations, large-scale personal information processors should also fulfill the special obligations stipulated in this clause. First, they should establish and perfect a personal information protection compliance system in accordance with national regulations and set up independent institutions by external members to supervise the protection of personal information, precisely auditing the technical ethical issues in their data innovation. Second, they should adhere to the principles of transparency, fairness, and impartiality and formulate platform guidelines that clarify the rights and obligations of different entities within the platform. This indeed aligns with Article 32 of the "E-commerce Law," which mandates that operators of e-commerce platforms must articulate the rights and obligations associated with gaining access to and withdrawing from the platform, guaranteeing the quality of goods and services, and safeguarding consumer's personal information, among other rights. By formulating platform rules and establishing the rights and obligations of all parties, it can complement external legal rules, thereby achieving the effect of pluralistic governance of Internet platforms. Third, should an entity within the platform seriously violate legal and administrative regulations pertaining to the processing of personal information while offering products or services, the platform is obligated to take immediate measures to halt the provision of such products or services by this entity. This is similar to the stipulation in Article 36 of the "E-commerce Law," aiming to have large internet platform operators supervise providers of products or services on their platforms. Finally, large-scale processors should regularly publish social responsibility reports on personal information protection, opening themselves up to public oversight. Considering the significant advantages that large-scale data processors have in terms of technology and information, their role should not be confined to serving their own interests. Instead, they ought to uphold legal, ethical, and various other societal responsibilities, fostering a positive and wholesome digital environment. Moreover, public oversight can effectively encourage large internet platform operators to focus more on their own governance practices, thereby enhancing the legality, security, and adherence to compliance standards in their handling of personal information.

32. 参见张新宝：《互联网生态"守门人"个人信息保护特别义务设置研究》，载《比较法研究》2021年第3期。Zhang Xinbao, "A Study on the Special Obligations of Personal Information Protection for the 'Gatekeepers' of the Internet Ecosystem," in "Comparative Law Research," 3 (2021).

§6. SPECIAL REGULATIONS FOR STATE ORGAN PROCESSORS

107. China adopts a unified legislative model for the regulation of personal information processing; that is, it does not distinguish between state authorities and non-state authorities but regulates them uniformly. This model was previously adopted in the "Cybersecurity Law" and the "Civil Code." When state organs act as personal information processors, however, their relationship with citizens is not equal and tends to be unilaterally coercive. How to incorporate the actions of state authorities in processing personal information into a legal framework is a significant challenge for personal information protection.[33]

108. In response to this, Articles 33 to 37 of the "Personal Information Protection Law" lay out the pertinent regulations for the role of state organs acting as processors. First of all, Article 33 makes it explicit that this law is applied to the legal use of personal information by state organs. Article 34 pertains to the general provisions for state authorities to process personal information in order to fulfill their statutory duties. The aim is to establish the powers and responsibilities of state authorities when processing personal information, ensuring that they must strictly process personal information within the scope of their powers and not exceed the necessary scope and limits. This article introduces three principles of rule of law in the activities of state authorities in processing personal information, namely, statutory authority, statutory procedure, and proportionality, in order to restrict the abuse of state power.[34] Article 35 stipulates the obligation of state authorities to inform individuals when processing their personal information, as well as situations where informing is not necessary. When state authorities process personal information in order to fulfill their statutory duties, in accordance with Article 13 of this law, they do not need to obtain personal consent. Nonetheless, the absence of a requirement for consent does not absolve state authorities from their obligation to notify. Notification is a prerequisite for ensuring an individual's right to be informed. Thus, whenever a state authority begins processing personal information, it is obligatory to notify the individual in question. Failing to do so may result in an abuse of power and violation of the individual's rights and interests. In exceptional circumstances, state authorities may be exempted from the obligation to inform. These mainly include situations where "laws and administrative regulations require confidentiality," as stipulated in Article 18, paragraph 1 of this law, such as personal information related to national security and state secrets. Other exceptions are cases where the act of informing would impede the state authorities from performing their statutory duties, such as collecting personal information from criminal suspects by public security authorities during criminal investigations. Article 36 stipulates that state authorities are obligated to store personal information domestically and to conduct

33. 参见王锡锌：《个人信息国家保护义务及展开》，载《中国法学》2021年第1期。Wang Xixin, "National Obligation to Protect Personal Information and Its Implementation," in "Chinese Jurisprudence," 1 (2021).

34. 参见龙卫球主编：《中华人民共和国个人信息保护法释义》，中国法制出版社2021年版，第162页 Long Weiqiu (ed.), "Interpretation of the Personal Information Protection Law of the People's Republic of China," (China Legal Publishing House 2021 edition), p. 162.

security assessments when providing it abroad. The law requires that state authorities store personal information within the country, indicating that China implements a data localization mechanism to prevent personal information from being stolen or leaked, thereby safeguarding personal information security and national security. Should there be a need to transmit personal information overseas, it is incumbent upon state authorities to perform a security evaluation of the information to be shared. However, as state authorities do not operate critical information infrastructure, they are not obliged to conduct a security assessment via the national cyberspace authority. Article 37 expands the scope of entities classified as state organs processing personal information, bringing organizations with public management functions authorized by laws and regulations, and other non-state authorities, into the same legal status as state organs. Provided these organizations carry out their legal obligations, they fall under the same provisions that govern state authorities' processing of personal information. Analogous stipulations can also be found in Article 43 of the "Data Security Law."

Part VI. Personal Information Security Standard System

109. In the digital age, personal information has evolved into a pivotal resource. The conflict between the protection and utilization of personal information is ubiquitous, presenting new challenges for the security protection of personal information. Personal information has characteristics completely different from traditional legal subjects. Most countries and international organizations lack adequate experience in dealing with this complex issue and are progressively navigating their way towards refining and perfecting the relevant legislation. However, the legal framework surrounding personal information security must grapple not only with the swiftly evolving landscape of digital technologies but also necessitates a timely overhaul of the imperfect legal systems currently in place. This is essential to reconcile the conflict between the protection and utilization of personal data. Law, in its narrower interpretation, wields a powerful compulsory force. However, it is this very force that necessitates its promulgation, amendment, and application to be subject to strict regulation. A degree of stability is indispensable in maintaining its solemnity and authority, thereby precluding the possibility of hasty alterations. In contrast, building a security standard system presents a more flexible and adaptable approach. This system can function effectively as an exploratory tool and a supportive pillar for the legislation.

110. China is establishing a vertical legal system for the protection of personal information security, ranging from the constitution, administrative law, criminal law to civil law, and a horizontal one from national security law, cybersecurity law, data security law to personal information protection law, it is also concurrently, or even ahead of time, establishing a large number of standards. From the perspective of the level of standards, it includes not only national standards, industry standards, and local standards led by the government but also "market standards" such as group standards and enterprise standards. In terms of the function of standards, it includes not only fundamental "basic requirement standards," "implementation guide standards," and "testing and assessment standards," but also "industry application standards" for various industries. Among these, the "basic requirement standards" stipulate the basic technical and management requirements for personal information security, which are applicable for guiding the construction, supervision, and management of personal information security. The "implementation guide standards" are a detailed explanation of the "basic requirement standards," thereby providing feasible guidance for achieving the requirements of personal information security.

The "testing and assessment standards" are established as executable, repeatable, and measurable testing methods, acceptance benchmarks, auditing rules, verification mechanisms for the implementation of the "basic requirement standard." The "industry application standards" are contextual regulations for the application of relevant standards in specific industries.

§1. National Standards and Technical Documents

111. In the field of personal information security, China has formulated nine national standards and technical documents, with several more national standards currently under development. These standards do not have mandatory force, but they provide effective references for the definition of terms: collection, storage, use, transfer, and deletion of personal information.

112. Classified as "basis requirement standards," "Information Security Technology—Personal Information Security Norms" (GB/T 35273-2020) is the most important national standard. It defines key concepts in personal information protection, such as personal information, sensitive personal information, explicit consent, and authorized consent through a method of definition + exemplification. It also provides the seven principles of personal information protection, and regulates personal information processing activities of various organizations from all aspects including collection, storage, use, entrusted processing, sharing, transfer, and public disclosure. Hence, this document offers an updated set of business benchmarks and behavioral guidelines, facilitating both corporate compliance and national regulation at a pragmatic operational level.

113. Other "basic requirement standards" in China include "Information Security Technology—Technical Requirements for the Protection of Personal Information in Mobile Intelligent Terminals" (GB/T 34978-2017), "Information Security Technology—Security Capability Requirements for Big Data Services" (GB/T35274-2017), "Requirements and Evaluation Methods for the Protection of Personal Information in Smart Home Appliances" (GB/T 40979-2021), and "Information Security Technology—Basic Requirements for Mobile Internet Applications (App) Collecting Personal Information" (GB/T 41391-2022). These documents make specific provisions for various sub-fields with significant demand, such as mobile intelligent terminals, big data services, smart home appliances, and Apps, among others.

114. In addition, "Information Security Technology—Guidelines for De-identification of Personal Information" (GB/T 37964-2019), "Information Technology—Security Techniques—Guide to Personal Information Protection in Public Clouds" (GB/T 41574-2022), and "Information Security Technology—Guide to Personal Information Protection in Public and Commercial Service Information Systems" (GB/Z 28828-2012) are all "implementation guide standards." The "Information Security Technology—Guide for Personal Information Security Impact

Assessment" (GB/T 39335-2020) falls under the category of "testing and assessment standards." They all belong to national standards and technical documents, providing detailed guidance for the implementation of "basic requirement standards" and the assessment of such implementation.

§2. Industry Standards and Group Standards

115. Industry standards for personal information security primarily focus on the telecommunications industry. They include the "Requirements for the Protection of Personal Information in Connected Vehicle Information Services" (YD/T 3746-2020); "Technical Requirements for Personal Information Protection in Mobile Browsers" (YD/T 3367-2018); "Technical Requirements for Personal Information Protection in Telecommunications and Internet Service Instant Messaging" (YD/T 3327-2018); "Technical Requirements for Personal Information Protection in Telecommunications and Internet Service E-commerce" (YD/T 3105-2016); "Technical Requirements for Personal Information Protection in Telecommunications and Internet Service Mobile Application Stores" (YD/T 3106-2016); "Technical Requirements for Personal Information Protection on Mobile Smart Terminals" (YD/T 3082-2016); "Definition and Classification of Personal Information Protection in Telecommunications and Internet Services" (YD/T 2781-2014); "Grading Guidelines for Personal Information Protection in Telecommunications and Internet Services" (YD/T 2782-2014); "Test Methods for Terminal Equipment in Mobile User Personal Information Management Services" (YD/T 2361-2011).

116. "Test Methods for System Equipment in Mobile User Personal Information Management Services" (YD/T 2131-2010); "Technical Requirements for System Equipment in Mobile User Personal Information Management Services" (YD/T 2130-2010); "General Technical Requirements for Mobile User Personal Information Management Services" (YD/T 2129-2010).

117. "Technical Requirements for Terminal Equipment in Mobile User Personal Information Management Services" (YD/T 2132-2010). These standards provide guidelines and requirements for the protection and management of personal information in various telecommunications and Internet services.

118. Other industries have also established their industry standards concerning personal information security. For instance, in the healthcare sector, there are standards such as "Health Record Sharing Document Specification Part 14: Registration of Personal Information for Patients with Severe Mental Disorders"(WS/T 483.14-2016), and "Basic Information Basic Dataset: Personal Information" (WS 371-2012). In the postal industry, standards like "Guidelines for Personal Information Protection of Postal Service Users" (YZ/T 0147-2015) and "Structure of Personal Information Database for Postal Use" (YZ/T 0002-2003) have been issued. In the field of public safety, there is the "Format for Arranging Personal Information for Visual Reading of Resident Identity Card" (GA 456-2004). In addition, the financial industry has introduced the "Chinese Financial Mobile Payment, Detection

Specification, Part 8: Personal Information Protection" (JR/T 0098.8-2012), and the electronic industry has promulgated the "Chinese Application Programming Interface Specification for Handheld Personal Information Processing Devices" (SJ/T 11229-2001).

119. It should be noted that the above industry standards were all implemented before the release of the "Personal Information Protection Law" in 2021. The earliest standards were even published and implemented as early as 2003, generally later than national standards and technical documents. These industry standards represent China's early exploration of personal information protection and form an important cornerstone of China's personal information protection practices.

120. In contrast to the industry standards that served as pioneers in personal information protection, it was only in 2017 that the revised "Standardization Law" established the legal status of group standards. At the same time as the establishment of the personal information legal framework, various organizations in the field of personal information security have been actively involved in the formulation of group standards. For example, the Telecommunication Terminal Industry Association has introduced the "Assessment Standard for the Minimum Necessary Collection of Personal Information by Apps, Section 5: Device Information" (T/TAF 077.5—2022) and "Implementation Guidelines for the Protection of Personal Information of Users of Mobile Intelligent Terminals and Application Software, Section 7: Targeted Push" (T/TAF 080—2021), among others. The China Software Industry Association has introduced the "Corporate Personal Information Security Management Standards" (T/SIA 001—2022). The China Association for Promotion of Cooperative Relations among Enterprises, Universities, and Research Institutes have developed the "Market Research: Personal Information Security Protection Requirements" (T/CAB 0101—2021). The China Science and Technology Law Society has formulated the Guidelines for the Legal Compliance Assessment of Personal Information Processing (T/CLAST 002—2021). These group standards cover various aspects such as personal information classification, informed consent, permission management, and application software privacy policies, contributing to the construction of personal information protection system.

Part VII. Rules for Cross-Border Provision of Personal Information

§1. General Requirements for Cross-Border Transfer of Personal Information

I. Separate Consent of the Subject of Personal Information

121. Under Article 39 of the Personal Information Protection Law, when the personal information processor provides personal information abroad, it is necessary to obtain the individual's separate consent. First, this consent must be based on sufficient disclosure; that is, the personal information processor needs to fulfill the necessary obligation to inform the individual. The specific scope of the information to be disclosed includes the overseas recipient's title or name, contact information, processing purpose, processing methods, types of personal information, along with the methods and procedures for individuals to exercise their rights provided in this law over the overseas recipient, among others. Second, this consent must be made in a specific way. Currently, the specific methods and implications of separate consent are not explicitly defined in the existing laws and regulations. It is only stipulated in the "Internet Data Security Management Regulations (Draft for Comments)" released by the National Cyberspace Administration that separate consent refers to the data processor obtaining personal consent for each piece of personal information when carrying out specific data processing activities, excluding one-time consent for multiple pieces of personal information and various processing activities.[35] In practice, the vague and unclear status of the legislation makes it difficult for relevant entities to fully implement the rules on obtaining separate consent for cross-border data transfer. It is thus necessary to formulate specific rules to address this problem in the future.

II. Requirements for the Pathway of Cross-Border Data Transfer

122. A prerequisite for the cross-border transfer of personal information is the assurance of the involved personal data's safety. According to Article 38 of the "Personal Information Protection Law," the criterion for determining whether personal

35. 《网络数据安全管理条例（征求意见稿）》第73条第8项。"Internet Data Security Management Regulations (Draft for Solicitation of Comments)," Art. 73, Item 8.

information can be transferred across borders is the level of equivalent protection. This means the data protection standards in the country or region where the overseas recipient of personal information is located must meet or exceed the personal information protection standards set forth by China's "Personal Information Protection Law." There are mainly three specific paths for fulfilling this requirement. First, per Article 40 of the "Personal Information Protection Law," the personal information processor passes the security assessment organized by the national cyberspace administration. Second, according to the regulations of the national cyberspace administration, the processor obtains the personal information protection certification through professional institutions. Third, in accordance with the standard contracts formulated by the national cyberspace administration, the processor establishes contracts with overseas recipients, outlining the rights and obligations of both parties. Additionally, the "Personal Information Protection Law" also sets a catch-all provision, that is, other paths or conditions stipulated by laws, administrative regulations, or the national cyberspace administration.

A. *Security Assessment for Across-Border Data Transfer*

123. According to Article 40 of the "Personal Information Protection Law," operators of critical information infrastructure and processors of personal information who reach the quantity stipulated by the national cyberspace administration should store personal information collected and generated within the territory of the People's Republic of China. If there is a need to provide information abroad, they should pass the security assessment organized by the national cyberspace administration. Critical information infrastructures include public communication and information services, power, traffic, water resources, finance, public service, e-government, and other critical information infrastructure which—if destroyed, suffering a loss of function, or experiencing leakage of data—might seriously endanger national security, national welfare, the people's livelihood, or the public interest.[36] Building upon the multitiered cybersecurity protection framework, the Chinese government enforces stringent safeguarding measures for these critical information infrastructures. This includes undertaking thorough security assessments for any cross-border transfers of personal information stored within these systems. Additionally, personal information processors dealing with a large quantity and scale of personal information also need to implement security assessment requirements. Specifically, these personal information processors include those processing personal information of more than 1 million individuals, those that have transferred personal information of 100,000 individuals to overseas recipients since January 1 of the previous year, and those processing sensitive personal information of 10,000 individuals within the same time frame.[37]

124. So far, China has issued the "Data Export Security Assessment Measures" and its supporting guidelines, the "Data Export Security Assessment Declaration

36. Article 31, para. 1 of the Cybersecurity Law.
37. Article 4 of the Data Export Security Assessment Measures.

Guide (First Edition)," forming a relatively complete legislative framework concerning data export security assessment procedures and evaluation standards. According to these two documents, the security assessment for the export of personal information must be conducted using a combination of "declaration assessment + self-assessment." The declaration assessment requires enterprises intending to conduct cross-border data transfers to submit an application to the provincial-level cyberspace department in the region where they are located. Following an initial review of document completeness by the provincial cyberspace department, the application is then forwarded to the National Cyberspace Administration for a substantial review and assessment. For both declaration assessment and self-assessment, the key assessment items encompass evaluating the legality, legitimacy, and necessity of data export activities, considering the influence of overseas legal and policy environments, assessing the scale, scope, type, and sensitivity of the exported data, analyzing the risks associated with data export, verifying if the data protection level of the overseas recipient meets an equivalent standard to that of China, ensuring sufficient protection and remedies for personal information rights, and reviewing if legal documents related to data export, such as contracts, adequately address data security protection responsibilities and obligations. However, there are also some slight differences between these two assessments. Specifically, as per the "Data Export Security Assessment Measures," the self-assessment conducted by enterprises does not encompass either the evaluation of the impact of overseas legal policy environments or the review of the compliance of the exporting party with Chinese laws, administrative regulations, and departmental rules.

B. Personal Information Protection Certification

125. The National Information Security Standardization Technical Committee has released the "Guidelines for Cybersecurity Standard Practices—Security Certification Specification for Cross-Border Processing of Personal Information" to provide guidance for professional organizations in conducting security certification for cross-border processing of personal information. According to this document, professional organization certification primarily applies to two scenarios. The first scenario involves cross-border processing of personal information between multinational companies or subsidiary or affiliated companies within the same economic or business entity. The second scenario involves personal information processing activities covered under Article 3, paragraph 2 of the "Personal Information Protection Law," which primarily refers to situations where overseas personal information processors handle personal information of individuals being located within China. It should be noted that conducting certification through professional organizations is a voluntary certification activity recommended by the government, rather than a mandatory requirement.

126. In the process of conducting personal information protection certification, there are several key requirements to consider. First, there must be legally binding agreements. This means that personal information processors and overseas recipients engaged in cross-border processing activities should sign legally binding and enforceable documents to ensure the full protection of the rights and interests of the individuals whose personal information is being processed. Second, there must be organizational management capabilities. This means that both the data exporting entity and the recipient entity must have dedicated personnel responsible for personal information protection and establish a personal information protection organization. Third, it is essential to comply with the rules for cross-border processing of personal information. This covers such specific aspects as the purpose, methods, and scope of such processing; the duration of storing personal information overseas and the procedures for handling it after expiration, the countries or regions involved in the cross-border data transfer, the resources and measures taken to protect the rights and interests of individuals whose information is being processed, and the rules for compensation and disposal in case of personal information security incidents. Fourth, it is necessary to conduct a personal information protection impact assessment. This assessment should be carried out before the data is transferred abroad to determine whether the activity of providing personal information overseas is legal, legitimate, and necessary and whether the protective measures taken are appropriate and effective in relation to the level of risk. Fifth, it is necessary to ensure the protection of the rights and interests of individuals whose personal information is being processed. This includes ensuring that individuals have specific rights regarding personal information protection and requiring both data exporting and receiving entities to assume corresponding responsibilities and obligations.

127. Although the certification specification establishes the basic framework for personal information protection certification, many specific rules for its implementation remain relatively vague. For instance, the specific certification organizations and their composition, as well as the detailed procedures for conducting the certification, are not yet clearly defined. However, in practice, there is a growing demand for professional organization certification on cross-border data transfer. It is foreseeable that more detailed rules will be formulated to meet this demand.

C. Standard Contract for Personal Information Export

128. The National Cyberspace Administration has released the "Standard Contract for Personal Information Export (Draft for Solicitation of Comments)," which includes specific applicable scenarios, related work procedures, and exemplary templates of the standard contract, among others. However, this legal document has not yet officially come into effect, and therefore there is still a lack of necessary compliance guidelines in practice.

129. According to this document, the standard contract can be applicable in scenarios when the following conditions are all satisfied: the data exporter is not an operator of critical information infrastructure; it processes personal information of fewer than 1 million individuals; since the beginning of the previous year, it has not provided personal information of 100,000 individuals to overseas entities; since the beginning of the previous year, it has not provided sensitive personal information of

10,000 individuals to overseas entities.[38] It can be seen that the applicability of the standard contract pathway is independent and mutually exclusive from the applicability of the security assessment pathway.

130. Prior to engaging in data export activities under standard contracts, the involved party should conduct a personal information protection impact assessment. Within ten working days after the standard contract comes into effect, the personal information processor should promptly file the standard contract text and the personal information protection impact assessment report with the provincial-level cyberspace department where they are located. When there are changes in circumstances, the personal information processor should promptly re-sign the standard contract and re-file it.

131. According to the relevant appendices of the draft for soliciting opinions, the standard contract should include basic information about the personal information processor and the overseas recipient, the basic situation of personal information export, responsibilities and obligations of the personal information processor and the overseas recipient to protect personal information, technical and management measures taken to prevent security risks that may arise from the export of personal information, the impact of the personal information protection laws and regulations in the country or region where the overseas recipient is located on the compliance with the terms of this contract, the rights of the personal information subject, and the measures to safeguard the rights of the personal information subject, relief approaches, contract termination, liability for breach of contract, dispute resolution, among others. In addition, the personal information processor and the overseas recipient can agree on other terms or sign other agreements regarding the export of personal information, but these must not conflict with the content of the standard contract.[39]

§2. Special Previsions of Cross-Border Transfer of Personal Information

I. Judicial and Law Enforcement Assistance

132. Both the "Data Security Law" and the "Personal Information Protection Law" stipulate that the competent authority shall handle requests from foreign judicial or law enforcement agencies for data provision, based on relevant laws and international treaties or agreements that China has signed or participated in, or in accordance with the principle of equality and reciprocity. Without the approval of the competent authority, organizations or individuals within the country must not

38. "Regulations on the Standard Contract for the Cross-border Transfer of Personal Information (Draft for Solicitation of Comments)," Art. 4.
39. "Regulations on the Standard Contract for the Cross-border Transfer of Personal Information (Draft for Solicitation of Comments)," Art. 2, Clause 2.

provide data stored in the country to foreign judicial or law enforcement agencies.[40] The primary legal basis for this is the "International Criminal Justice Assistance Law," which stipulates the main circumstances in which the competent authority can provide cross-border judicial assistance.[41] The international treaties and agreements as the basis of cross-border data transfer refers to bilateral or multilateral judicial or law enforcement assistance agreements that China has entered into with foreign countries. When such treaties or agreements do not exist, the situation should be handled based on the diplomatic principle of equality and reciprocity. If such assistance would damage national sovereignty, security, or the public interest, it should be not provided.[42] In addition, the provision of cross-border data for judicial or law enforcement assistance should only involve relevant state power authorities. In cases where private organizations or individuals are involved in the cross-border data transfer, whether they are proactively initiating lawsuits, responding to legal actions, or undergoing law enforcement investigations, they must first obtain approval from the domestic judicial or law enforcement agencies. Only then can they supply data to foreign entities for the purposes of law enforcement or judicial proceedings. According to the "International Criminal Justice Assistance Law," the state power authorities mentioned here mainly include the National Supervisory Commission, the Supreme People's Court, the Supreme People's Procuratorate, the Ministry of Public Security, and the Ministry of State Security among others.[43]

II. Blacklist System

133. According to Article 42 of the "Personal Information Protection Law," if foreign organizations or individuals engage in activities related to the processing of

40. "Data Security Law," Art. 36; "Personal Information Protection Law," Art. 41.
41. Article 2 of the "International Criminal Judicial Assistance Law," stipulates: "The international criminal judicial assistance referred to in this Law means the mutual assistance provided by the People's Republic of China and foreign countries in activities such as investigation, inquiry, prosecution, trial, and execution of criminal cases. This includes serving documents, investigating and collecting evidence, arranging for witnesses to testify or assisting in investigations, sealing, seizing, freezing involved assets, confiscating, returning illegal gains and other involved assets, transferring sentenced individuals, and other forms of assistance."
42. 参见程啸：《个人信息保护法理解与适用》，中国法制出版社2021年版，第322－323页。Cheng Xiao, "Understanding and Application of the Personal Information Protection Law," (China Legal Publishing House 2021 edition), pp. 322–323.
43. Article 6 of the "International Criminal Judicial Assistance Law," stipulates: "The National Supervisory Commission, the Supreme People's Court, the Supreme People's Procuratorate, the Ministry of Public Security, and the Ministry of State Security are the competent authorities responsible for carrying out international criminal judicial assistance. Based on their respective duties, they review criminal judicial assistance requests made to foreign countries and examine and handle criminal judicial assistance requests from foreign entities relayed by external liaison bodies. They also undertake other tasks related to international criminal judicial assistance. In cases involving the transfer of sentenced individuals, the Ministry of Justice assumes the corresponding responsibilities of the competent authorities based on its division of duties. The agencies handling cases related to criminal judicial assistance are the working institutions for international criminal judicial assistance. They are responsible for submitting requests for criminal judicial assistance to foreign countries to their respective competent authorities and executing criminal judicial assistance requests from foreign countries as assigned by their competent authorities."

personal information that infringe upon the rights and interests of Chinese citizens' personal information, or endanger national security and public interests of China, the national cyberspace administration has the authority to list them on a restricted or banned personal information supply list, make an announcement to the public, and take measures to restrict or ban the supply of personal information to them.

III. Principle of Reciprocity

134. According to Article 43 of the Personal Information Protection Law, any country or region that adopts discriminatory prohibitions, restrictions, or other similar measures against the People's Republic of China in terms of personal information protection, China may take reciprocal measures against that country or region based on the actual situation. This article is factually a legal response by China to the relevant international circumstances. For example, U.S. President Joe Biden issued an executive order requiring the Committee on Foreign Investment in the United States (CFIUS) to conduct security reviews of cross-border data transactions. If it determines that such transactions pose a threat to U.S. national security, the CFIUS possesses the authority to mandate the suspension of pertinent cross-border transactions and may even require foreign companies to divest their operations conducted within the United States. Similarly, the United States Congress enacted the Foreign Investment Risk Review Modernization Act of 2018 (FIRRMA), which establishes a national security review mechanism for foreign investments in critical infrastructure and sensitive personal information sectors within the country. The CFIUS takes the lead in administering this mechanism. Given this international context, enacting the principle of reciprocity through legislation carries clear practical significance for China, especially when considering the implementation of necessary countermeasures.

Part VIII. Performance of Personal Information Protection Duties

§1. Departments Performing Personal Information Protection Duties

135. The departments fulfilling personal information protection duties refer to state authorities that bear personal information protection and supervisory management responsibilities according to laws, administrative regulations, and relevant state provisions. Specifically, Article 60 of the "Personal Information Protection Law" stipulates: (i) The National Cyberspace Administration is responsible for overall coordination of personal information protection work and related supervision and management work. Relevant departments of the State Council, in accordance with this law and relevant laws and administrative regulations, are responsible for personal information protection and supervision and management work within their respective scope of responsibilities; (ii) The responsibilities for personal information protection and supervision and management of relevant departments of local governments at or above the county level are determined in accordance with relevant national regulations. Similarly, Article 8 of the "Cybersecurity Law" stipulates: (i) The National Cyberspace Administration is responsible for the overall coordination of cybersecurity work and related supervision and management work. The State Council's telecommunication regulatory department, public security departments, and other relevant authorities, in accordance with this law and relevant laws and administrative regulations, are responsible for cybersecurity protection and supervision and management work within their respective scope of responsibilities; (ii) The responsibilities for cybersecurity protection and supervision and management of relevant departments of local governments at or above the county level are determined in accordance with relevant national regulations. Therefore, the departments in China that fulfill the responsibilities of personal information protection include the National Cyberspace Administration; departments stipulated by relevant laws and administrative regulations, such as the State Council's telecommunications regulatory department and public security department; and relevant departments of local governments at or above the county level.

136. Specifically, the main duties of the National Cyberspace Administration include: (1) Cybersecurity oversight: it is responsible for formulating and implementing policies related to cybersecurity, safeguarding national and information security in the cyberspace domain; (2) Internet content management: it oversees and manages internet content within China. It formulates guidelines and regulations related to the dissemination of information on the internet. It aims to maintain control over online content, ensuring it aligns with the Chinese government's guidelines and censorship policies; (3) Regulation of Internet Services: It provides overall coordination and guidance for internet services across the country. It formulates policies to promote the healthy development of the Internet industry, encourages technological innovation, and ensures compliance with relevant laws and regulations; (4) Online media regulation: it is responsible for supervising online media platforms, including news websites, social media platforms, and video-sharing platforms. It enforces strict licensing requirements and content regulations for online media entities; (5) Data protection and privacy: it plays a role in formulating and implementing data protection and privacy policies. It works to ensure the security of personal information and data collected and processed by internet companies operating within China; and (6) International cooperation and cyber diplomacy: it engages in international cooperation on cybersecurity issues. It participates in global discussions, negotiations, and initiatives related to cyberspace governance and cybersecurity, representing China's interests in the international arena.

137. The State Council's telecommunications regulatory department currently refers mainly to the Ministry of Industry and Information Technology. Its main responsibilities include formulating and implementing industry plans, industrial policies, and standards; monitoring the daily operation of the industry; promoting the development of major technical equipment and independent innovation; managing the communications industry; guiding the advancement of informatization construction; and coordinating to maintain national information security, etc. The State Council's public security department mainly refers to the Ministry of Public Security. According to Article 6, paragraph 3 of the "Data Security Law," it is responsible for undertaking data security supervision within their respective responsibilities. Article 6, paragraph 1 of the "Regulations on the Security Protection of Computer Information Systems" also stipulates that "The Ministry of Public Security is responsible for the national computer information system security protection work." In addition, Article 6, paragraph 2 of the "Data Security Law" stipulates: "The industrial, telecommunications, transportation, financial, natural resources, health, education, and science and technology authorities undertake the data security supervision duties in their respective industries and fields." This mainly involves ministries and commissions such as the China Banking and Insurance Regulatory Commission, China Securities Regulatory Commission, People's Bank of China, Ministry of Natural Resources, National Health Commission, Ministry of Education, and Ministry of Science and Technology, among others. Each ministry and commission performs its own duties, managing personal information protection issues within its own regulatory field. Relevant departments of local governments at or above the county level are not specifically stipulated by law. This is mainly because the settings of local governments at different levels are varied, and the scope of personal information protection and supervision work is very broad. Therefore, their duties should be determined in accordance with the actual conditions on the ground, aligning with national laws, administrative regulations, departmental rules, and the normative documents issued by the relevant supervisory authorities.

§2. DEPARTMENTS' DUTIES AND MEASURES TO FULFILL DUTIES

138. Article 61 of the "Personal Information Protection Law" provides a general provision on the duties of the departments responsible for personal information protection, mainly divided into four aspects: publicity & supervision, protection, evaluation, and handling. With respect to the publicity and supervision duties, each department operates within its own sphere, guided by the obligations delineated in relevant laws and regulations. For instance, the cyberspace administration department is responsible for public education and advocacy efforts surrounding the protection of minors' personal information whilst also overseeing how personal user information is safeguarded by entities such as live streaming platforms, online game operators, and social media networks. The protection duty requires supervisory departments to investigate whether personal information processors have violated laws and administrative regulations when handling personal information based on the complaints and reports they receive. The evaluation duty requires relevant departments to organize inspections and assessments of how Apps and other processors handle personal information protection. The handling duty requires relevant departments to investigate and verify any violations of related laws and administrative regulations by personal information processors and to punish them in accordance with specific legal and regulatory requirements. For example, Article 79 of the "E-Commerce Law" stipulates: "E-commerce operators who violate laws and administrative regulations related to personal information protection, or fail to fulfill the network security obligations stipulated in Article 30 of this law and relevant laws and administrative regulations, shall be punished in accordance with the provisions of the 'Cybersecurity Law and other laws and administrative regulations.'

139. In order to better fulfill their responsibilities, departments in charge of personal information protection need to have corresponding law enforcement powers. Therefore, Article 63 of the "Personal Information Protection Law" specifically lists the law enforcement measures that these departments can take and requires the parties involved to assist and cooperate, and they should not refuse or obstruct. It is worth noting that when the relevant departments perform their duties, they must follow the procedures and specific requirements stipulated by administrative law to avoid illegal behavior. For example, when implementing administrative coercive actions such as sealing up and confiscation, administrative organs should adhere to the following provisions stipulated in Article 18 of the "Administrative Compulsory Law": (1) they must report to the person in charge of the administrative organ and get approval before implementation; (2) the measures should be implemented by two or more administrative law enforcement officers; (3) the law enforcement identification must be shown; (4) the parties involved should be notified to attend; (5) the parties should be informed on the spot of the reasons and basis for taking administrative compulsory measures, as well as the rights they are legally entitled to and the ways of relief; (6) the statement and defense of the parties should be heard; (7) an on-site record should be made; (8) the on-site record should be signed or stamped by the parties and the administrative law enforcement officers. If the parties refuse, it should be noted in the record; (9) if the parties do not attend, witnesses should be invited to attend and sign or stamp the on-site record together with the administrative law enforcement officers; (10) other procedures stipulated by laws and regulations.

140. Article 64 of the "Personal Information Protection Law" stipulates two measures: mandatory interview and mandatory compliance audits. Mandatory interview mainly refers to the administrative organ inviting the supervised individual or entity for a talk, providing instruction, or issuing warnings when there is a risk of violation or a minor violation has already occurred. The aim is to suggest the supervised to correct their unlawful actions and prevent them from engaging in activities that carry the risk of violation. Mandatory compliance auditing is the enforced procedure that arises when high-risk activities are identified in the handling of personal information or following a security breach involving such data. In such situations, the responsible administrative authority has the power to insist that the personal information handlers engage a professional institution to undertake a compliance audit of their personal information processing activities. In addition, Article 65 of the "Personal Information Protection Law" grants any organization or individual the right to complain or report, which enables the relevant regulatory authorities to more efficiently and comprehensively discover illegal activities that violate personal information protection.

§3. Legal Liability

I. Administrative Penalties for Illegal Processing of Personal Information

141. Articles 66 and 67 of the "Personal Information Protection Law" primarily stipulate specific penalty measures and the inclusion of credit records. Article 68 mainly prescribes the punishment for state organs that fail to fulfill their obligations of personal information protection. Article 66 distinguishes two types of circumstances: "ordinary" and "serious." However, it does not specifically define what constitutes "ordinary" or "serious" circumstances. As a result, determining the classification while applying this legal provision becomes a challenging task. In general, the distinction between the two will be made based on a comprehensive assessment of factors such as the number of violations, the severity of the consequences, and the degree of intentional malice. Article 67 mentions documenting the illegal acts in credit records and making them public, a method known as the "dishonesty punishment." This term refers to a system that uses administrative, economic, industry management, and public opinion means to impose warnings, restrictions, and constraints on individuals or entities listed in the dishonesty list. The credit record mentioned in the article is an essential part of China's social credit system construction. It refers to the credit data pertaining to individuals or organizations that is compiled, archived, and analyzed by governmental entities or credit reporting agencies. This credit record reflects the credibility and public trustworthiness of individuals and corporations in their market transactions. It functions as a vital piece of evidence and provides the groundwork for evaluating the honesty, trustworthiness, legality, and absence of illicit or deceptive actions of individuals or organizations. It forms the foundation for issuing credit reports and implementing credit disciplinary measures. Such a punitive mechanism cannot only serve as an administrative penalty to regulate the behavior of personal information handlers but also utilize public opinion supervision to engage individuals and social organizations in the realm of personal information protection. This expands the regulatory purview and strengthens regulatory efforts.

142. Article 68 specifically stipulates the corresponding punitive measures for state organs that fail to fulfill their obligations to protect personal information. State organs, due to their duties, often hold a vast amount of personal information. Any instances of information breaches or losses cannot only harm individual citizens' interests but also have the potential to jeopardize the public interests at large, affecting social order and national security. Therefore, the "Personal Information Protection Law" has specifically stipulated related punitive measures, aiming to strengthen the management, supervision, and constraints on state organs involved in the protection of personal information.

II. Liability and Civil Remedies for the Infringement of Personal Information Rights

143. Article 69 of the "Personal Information Protection Law" stipulates: "If the processing of personal information infringes upon personal information rights and causes damage, and the personal information processor cannot prove that they are not at fault, they should bear the liability for damages and other tort liabilities. The liability for compensation mentioned in the previous paragraph is determined according to the losses suffered by the individual or the benefits gained by the personal information processor as a result; if the losses suffered by the individual and the benefits gained by the personal information processor are difficult to determine, the amount of compensation will be determined according to the actual circumstances. The first paragraph of this article makes 'causing damage' a necessary condition for bearing the liability for compensation for the infringement of personal information rights. Meanwhile, Article 1166 of the 'Civil Code' stipulates: "if the actor causes damage to the civil rights and interests of others, regardless of whether the actor is at fault, if the law stipulates that they should bear the liability for the tort, it shall be done in accordance with such provisions." It means that the "Personal Information Protection Law'" adopts a system of presumed fault liability for addressing compensation for infringement. This approach serves two primary functions. First, it alleviates the burden of proof on the victim, thereby enhancing the protection of personal information rights. Second, when compared to a no-fault liability system, fault liability offers the personal information processor the chance to prove their lack of fault and thereby potentially absolve themselves of responsibility. Thus, the application of the fault liability principle intends to strikes a balance between fortifying personal information protection and preserving the legal rights of personal information processors. The second paragraph of this article defines the method for determining the benefits of liability for compensation for damages, including the losses suffered by the individual, the benefits gained by the personal information processor as a result, and in cases where it is difficult to determine, the compensation amount is decided based on the actual circumstances. In practice, the above determination methods often face issues with specific confirmation, such as how to determine the specific amount of compensation liability for damage to reputation caused by personal information leaks. Therefore, how to apply this law in practice still requires analysis and consideration through case studies.

III. Administrative Penalties and Criminal Liability for Unlawful Processing of Personal Information

144. Article 71 of the "Personal Information Protection Law" stipulates: where any violation of this law constitutes a breach of public security administration, administrative penalties shall be imposed according to law; if it constitutes a crime, criminal liability shall be pursued according to law. Given that the "Public Security Administration Punishments Law" underwent revision in 2012, it currently lacks specific provisions regarding administrative penalties for unlawful handling of personal information. Therefore, how to apply public security administration penalties to deal with public security issues related to unlawful processing of personal information requires further legal improvements.

145. The Chinese Criminal Law stipulates the Crime of Infringing Citizens' Personal Information. According to Article 253a, whoever, in violation of the relevant provisions of the State, sells or provides others with citizens' personal information, if the circumstances are serious, shall be sentenced to fixed-term imprisonment of not more than three years or criminal detention, and/or be fined; if the circumstances are especially serious, he shall be sentenced to fixed-term imprisonment of not less than three years but not more than seven years, and be fined. Whoever, in violation of the relevant provisions of the State, sells or provides others with the citizens' personal information obtained during the course of performing duties or providing services shall be given a heavier punishment in accordance with the preceding paragraph. Whoever illegally obtains the above-mentioned information by theft or otherwise shall be punished in accordance with the provisions of paragraph 1. Where an organization commits any of the crimes mentioned in the preceding three paragraphs, it shall be fined, and the persons directly in charge of the organization and other persons directly liable shall be punished in accordance with the respective provisions of the preceding three paragraphs.

IV. Comments

146. Generally speaking, the "Personal Information Protection Law" marks China's first legislation concerning personal information and has laid a robust foundation for fulfilling the responsibility of safeguarding personal data. It fills the legal gaps on relevant issues, carries significant importance, and possesses a certain level of practicability. However, there are still many shortcomings that urgently need to be improved. For instance, regarding the departments responsible for fulfilling personal information protection duties, the challenges lie in the existence of numerous and chaotic managing departments and the lack of a well-organized leadership framework. These issues may result in problems like overlapping or ambiguous jurisdictions in the implementation of personal information protection. Regarding the responsibilities of various departments and the measures they can adopt to fulfill these duties, there is a lack of detailed explanations of specific situations. For example, it does not provide a clear definition of what qualifies as a "significant risk in the processing of personal information." In addition, the stipulations under the "Personal Information Protection Law" need to be applied in conjunction with other laws, such as civil law, administrative law, and criminal law. However, due to China's relatively late attention to legal issues concerning personal information protection, the existing legal system faces challenges in effectively filling the gaps associated with the "Personal Information Protection Law." For example, the "Personal Information Protection Law" stipulates that violations of public security management should be subject to legal punishment in accordance with the law. However, the "Public Security Administration Punishments Law" does not include any provisions specifically addressing personal information protection, creating a challenging situation when applying the law in such cases. Similarly, in the section of legal liability, the "Personal Information Protection Law" stipulates escalated penalties for serious violations of its provisions in processing personal information. However, it fails to provide a clear definition of what qualifies as "serious" violations, leaving room for ambiguity and potential inconsistencies in enforcement. However, as the enforcement of the "Personal Information Protection Law" strengthens after its promulgation, the number of related cases will increase, and related experience will accumulate. As a result, relevant legal gaps are expected to be filled through judicial practice, thus constructing a more detailed and rigorous legal framework for the protection of personal information.

Part IX. Special Scenarios for Personal Information Processing

147. In addition to processing personal information based on "personal consent," personal information processors can also process personal information based on statutory permission. Personal information essentially carries personal interests, public interests, and national interests, so personal information should not be entirely controlled by individuals. The law allows personal information processors to carry out personal information processing activities in certain circumstances without obtaining personal consent. Unlike the right to life, health, and physical integrity, the determination of the protection boundary for personal information rights is actually a dynamic balancing process. When it involves the legitimate interests of others, public interests, or national interests, the law needs to place restrictions on the rights and interests related to personal information. The reasonable use of personal information contributes to the development of the digital economy, as well as enhancing social governance and national governance capabilities. Starting from maintaining public interests and ensuring social production and life, Chinese law stipulates some statutory reasons for personal information processing, which are specifically reflected in the following typical scenarios.

§1. Processing Based on News, Academic, Artistic, or Literary Expression

148. The personal information of individuals can be appropriately utilized for activities in the public interest such as news reporting and public opinion supervision. However, if this use is unreasonable and infringes upon the personal rights of these individuals, they are required to assume legal responsibility in accordance with the law. The issue that needs to be reconciled is the tension between the freedom of expression and the protection of personal information. The Constitution of China upholds the freedom of speech as stated in Article 35, affirming that Chinese citizens have the freedom of speech, publication, assembly, association, march, and demonstration. News reporting plays an important role in public opinion supervision, contributing to the exercise of individuals' rights. Citizens can leverage news media to voice criticisms and provide suggestions to public authorities, public servants and on matters of public affairs. This represents not only an expression of free speech but also a mechanism for public participation in public affairs. In the process of news reporting, personal information of natural persons may be used. However, instances of personal information violations can also occur in this context. The law needs to draw a clear boundary between news reporting and the protection of personal information. According to Article 13 of the "Personal Information Protection Law" and Article 999 of the "Civil Code," if news reporting is for the purpose of protecting public interest, the news media can legally process personal information without obtaining personal consent, but it should be within a reasonable range.

149. In addition to news reporting, personal information processors do not need to obtain personal consent when reasonably processing personal information in situations such as scientific research and artistic appreciation. While Article 999 of the "Civil Code" specifically enumerates just two activities, namely news reporting and public opinion supervision, the inclusion of the term "etc." afterwards implies a provision for other circumstances to potentially constitute legal grounds for information processing. Referring to Article 1020 of the "Civil Code," no personal consent is required for the use of personal information within the necessary range for personal learning, art appreciation, classroom teaching, scientific research, and literary expression. These activities all have certain public interest attributes and take precedence over personal information protection.

§2. Public Disclosure of Governmental Data by State Agencies

150. When state agencies are required to collect and utilize data to perform their legal obligations, they must operate within the confines of their legal jurisdiction, adhering to the conditions and protocols prescribed by laws and administrative regulations. The management of personal information by these state agencies principally involves two stages: the collection and disclosure of personal information.

151. Personal information collected by state agencies is generally integrated into government data. State agencies not only include administrative bodies but also legislative and judicial bodies, among other public authorities. State agencies collect personal information under various scenarios and for different purposes, and the legal justifications for doing so vary accordingly. Under normal circumstances, state agencies need to follow the principle of informed consent when collecting personal information, and they must obtain the consent of the individual. Under specific circumstances, however, state agencies can collect personal information without obtaining individual consent. As per Article 13 of the "Personal Information Protection Law," "the necessity to fulfill statutory duties and obligations" is considered one of the legitimate reasons for processing personal information. Relevant laws have made provisions for the processing of personal information by state agencies in the performance of their statutory duties. For example, Article 7 of the "Exit and Entry Administration Law" states that, with the approval of the State Council, the Ministry of Public Security and the Ministry of Foreign Affairs can make regulations on the collection of biometric information, such as fingerprints, of individuals entering and leaving the country, according to the needs of exit and entry administration. Article 3 of the "Resident Identity Card Law" delineates that the data registered on a resident identity card should comprise the following: name, gender, ethnicity, date of birth, address of permanent residence, identity number, personal photograph, fingerprint information, document's validity period, and the issuing authority. In the aforementioned scenarios, state agencies undertake their statutory obligations in order to uphold national security, safeguard public interest, and protect the legitimate rights and interests of relevant individuals and organizations. Some of these actions even necessitate limiting citizens' rights and freedoms. These measures are compulsory and, in these instances, the collection of personal information should not, and indeed cannot, hinge upon the procurement of individual consent as a precondition for legality. When determining whether a state agency's collection of personal information has a legal basis, two key points need to be considered. First, the state agency is performing its statutory duties. The source of these statutory duties is not limited to laws and administrative regulations, but requires a comprehensive judgment based on relevant factors. Local regulations, departmental regulations, and local government regulations may also form the normative basis for statutory duties. Second, the collection of personal information must be necessary for the performance of statutory duties. This collection can either constitute the entirety of the act or be an integral component of it. Both scenarios are in accordance with the principle of necessity. The former scenario could include the collection of personal data by national statistical bodies in line with the "Statistics Law," whereas the latter could encompass the accumulation of personal information in relation to specific administrative actions, such as filing declarations and enforcing penalties.

152. State agencies need to disclose government data in accordance with the law. As per Article 41 of the "Data Security Law," state agencies should follow the principles of fairness, justice, and convenience, and disclose government data in a timely and accurate manner as prescribed by law, except for cases where disclosure is not permitted by law. It should be noted that the disclosure of government data is different from the disclosure of government information. According to Article 2 of the "Regulations on the Disclosure of Government Information," government information refers to information that administrative organs have produced or obtained in the process of performing administrative management functions and recorded and stored in a certain form. Examples include reports, press releases, speeches, legislation, regulations, policies, guidelines, and official communications. There is no general definition of government data in regulatory documents. It usually refers to raw, unprocessed, or minimally processed statistics, facts, and figures collected, generated, or held by the government. Examples include census data, public health data, economic statistics, environmental measures, and crime statistics. Government data is usually more granular and requires some interpretation or analysis to be useful or meaningful. The act of disclosing government information and government data each serve different purposes. The disclosure of government information primarily aims to provide oversight on the legality of administrative operations, acting as a bulwark against misuse of public authority. Meanwhile, the objective of revealing government data is to stimulate data sharing and enhance its effective utilization. Guided by the principles of justice, fairness, and convenience, state agencies should adopt uniform standards and rules when releasing government data. They should treat all entities equally, simplify the data provision procedures, and promote fair and efficient use of the data. However, in the process of making government data accessible, how and whether to open up government data that contains personal information is still under exploration. China's "Personal Information Protection Law" does not differentiate between private and public entities as personal information processors. In principle, public entities are also required to comply with the general provisions of the "Personal Information Protection Law." Local governments have attempted to make some provisions in this regard. For instance, the "Interim Measures for the Opening of Public Data in Shanghai" consider that the protection of personal information is a factor that influences data classification and categorization. As a result, public data that encompasses commercial secrets, personal privacy, or data that laws and regulations prohibit from being disclosed are classified as non-open data. This non-open data is only subject to disclosure under specific conditions such as legal declassification or de-identification, or if the relevant rights holder consents to its release. Once these conditions are met, the data can be reclassified as either unconditionally open data or conditionally open data.

§3. Courts Releasing Judicial Documents on the Internet

153. In 2000, the Supreme People's Court enacted the "Measures on Publication of Judicial Documents," ushering in an era of orderly disclosure of these documents. This practice of releasing judicial documents contributes significantly to the court's ongoing efforts to enhance judicial transparency and sustain judicial impartiality. As reported by the People's Court Newspaper, the China Judgments Online website surpassed a significant milestone as of August 30, 2020, with the total number of available documents exceeding 100 million and the site garnering nearly 48 billion cumulative visits. The judicial documents provide considerable benefits in facilitating consistent judgments in analogous cases, aiding in trial proceedings, and serving as a rich resource for academic research. Judicial documents generally contain personal information of subjects such as the plaintiff, defendant, accused, and witnesses, which is a necessary part of the judicial documents. As per Article 13 of the "Personal Information Protection Law," the Court holds the statutory right to collect and process personal information without the consent of the involved individuals. Consequently, the public accessibility of these judicial documents often signifies that the personal data within them are made available to the general public. Therefore, the value of making judicial documents public is in contradiction with the protection of personal information. It's important to find a reasonable scope and limit for the public disclosure of judicial documents.

154. Typically, regardless of whether a court has redacted part of the personal information in its judgment documents, it still falls under the regulation of the "Personal Information Protection Law." The "Regulation of the Supreme People's Court on Releasing Judgement Documents on the Internet" adopts anonymization techniques for three types of cases: marriage, family & inheritance disputes, criminal cases, and cases involving minors. The so-called anonymization technique refers to retaining the surname and replacing the given name with "X"; for ethnic minority names, the first character is kept while the rest are replaced with "X"; for Chinese translations of names of foreigners or stateless individuals, the first character is retained and the rest are replaced with "X"; for English names of foreigners or stateless individuals, the first English letter is retained and the rest is deleted. However, this kind of anonymization does not completely equate to anonymization under the "Personal Information Protection Law." Anonymization in the context of the law refers to a process whereby personal information is processed to the point where it's impossible to identify a specific individual and this process is irreversible. Regarding the published judgment documents, in cases with relatively rich details, sometimes combining these details with the surname can still lead to the identification of a specific individual. As it pertains to the published judgment documents, there are instances where even with the partial anonymization of names, the rich details within the case narrative could be combined with the retained surname and potentially lead to the identification of specific individuals. Therefore, when judgement documents are released to the public, it's imperative that they align with the provisions of the "Personal Information Protection Law." In particular, sensitive personal information must be removed from these documents to ensure privacy protection. According to Article 28 of the "Personal Information Protection Law," sensitive personal information is information that, once leaked or illegally used, could potentially harm the individual's personal dignity or endanger their personal or property safety. This includes information such as biometric identification, religious beliefs, specific identities, medical health, financial accounts, tracking data, as well as the personal information of minors under the age of 14. Sensitive personal information can only be processed when there is a specific purpose and sufficient necessity, and strict protective measures are also in place. Therefore, Article 10 of the "Provisions of the Supreme People's Court on Releasing Judgement Documents on the Internet" stipulates that when a court releases judgement documents on the Internet, it should remove personal information such as the individual's home address, contact information, identification card number, bank account number, health status, license plate number, and numbers of movable or immovable property ownership certificates. It can be seen that the practice of anonymizing personal names and eliminating sensitive personal information purports to strike a balance between safeguarding public interest and preserving individual privacy.

§4. Employers Processing Employee Personal Information

155. When employers carry out human resource management, they often need to process the personal information of workers, especially in situations like signing labor contracts, managing labor, handling social security documents, and providing professional training. Article 13 of the "Personal Information Protection Law" provides a separate provision, stating that the necessary processing of personal information for human resource management, in accordance with legally established labor rules and legally signed collective contracts, is a separate legitimate reason in the context of personal information processing.

156. The employer's handling of employees' personal information should not rely solely on the principle of informed consent. On one hand, the unequal relationship between employees and employers determines that informed consent does not have applicable space. On the other hand, the employer has a legitimate interest in handling necessary personal information for human resource management; thus the processing of personal information should not be controlled by the individual. Informed consent must be voluntarily given by the individual, the implied premise being that the individual and the personal information processor are on equal footing. However, the hierarchical relationship between employees and employers, characterized by managerial oversight, casts doubt on the nature of consent requested by employers. It remains unclear whether such consent is merely a reflection of managerial directives or whether it genuinely aims to acquire the voluntary agreement of the employee. When employees decide not to consent, they are very likely to face negative consequences, further proving that consent under labor relations cannot truly be given voluntarily. However, employers need to rely on the processing of personal information to ensure the smooth operation of human resource management. This not only involves the contractual obligations of the employees but also the legal obligations of the employers. Specifically, Article 8 of the "Labor Contract Law" stipulates that the employer has the right to know the basic situation directly related to the labor contract of the worker, and the worker should state it truthfully. Article 58 of the "Social Insurance Law" stipulates that the employer should apply for social insurance registration with the social insurance administration agency for its workers within thirty days from the date of employment. If the social insurance registration is not carried out, the social insurance administration agency is responsible for establishing the amount of social insurance premiums that should be paid. These all require the employer to process the personal information of the worker, and the employer has a legitimate interest in doing so.

157. The processing of personal information necessary for implementing human resource management should be based on legally established labor rules and regulations or legally signed collective contracts. The "Labor Contract Law" stipulates the procedures for formulating labor rules and regulations and signing collective contracts. When establishing, adjusting, or making decisions on rules or significant issues that directly impact workers' primary interests—including matters such as labor remuneration, work schedules, rest periods and vacations, workplace safety and sanitation, insurance benefits, employee training, labor discipline, and labor quota management—employers should engage in discussions with the workers' representative assembly or all employees, and the final determinations should be reached through equitable consultations with the union or employee representatives.

§5. Processing in Response to Public Health Emergencies

158. Public health emergencies refer to events that occur unexpectedly and cause or potentially cause serious harm to public health. These include major infectious disease outbreaks, mass unexplained illnesses, major food and occupational poisoning, and other events that seriously affect public health. Major infectious disease outbreaks are one type of public health incident. These outbreaks concern the public interest and affect the safety of people's lives and health. In such circumstances, it is neither scientific nor feasible to require personal information processing to obtain individual consent. The safety of people's lives and health ranks significantly higher in value than the protection of personal information. Also, the principle of informed consent is not compatible with the timeliness needed to respond to sudden incidents. Article 13 of the Personal Information Protection Law identifies the necessity to respond to public health emergencies on a separate lawful basis. In such cases, the processing of personal information does not require the consent of the individual.

159. The adequate collection of epidemic information forms the basis for epidemic prediction and warning, isolation control, and understanding of the transmission chain. The big data analysis based on this plays an important role in epidemic prevention and control. The law grants disease control and other institutions the power to process personal information. For example, Article 12 of the "Infectious Disease Prevention and Control Law" stipulates that all units and individuals within China must accept the investigation, inspection, sample collection, isolation treatment, and other prevention and control measures related to infectious diseases by disease control and medical institutions, and truthfully provide relevant information. Under Article 40 of the Regulations on Response to Public Health Emergencies, during the outbreak and spread of infectious diseases, local community organizations like street offices, townships, residents' committees, and villagers' committees should rally resources, unite, and collaborate. They should undertake community-based preventative measures and treatments, assist health administrative departments, other relevant agencies, and medical institutions in the collection and reporting of epidemic information. They should also aid in the isolation of affected individuals, carry out public health measures, and disseminate knowledge about the prevention and control of infectious diseases to residents and villagers. Although the processing of personal information in response to sudden public health emergencies does not require individual consent, it does not exempt the processors of personal information from their other obligations. Moreover, the processing of personal information in such cases is still subject to the principle of necessity, and the scope and method of personal information processing must not exceed reasonable limits.

Part X. Special Systems for Personal Information Protection

§1. Confidentiality System for Personal Information

160. In our modern society, state agencies often collect personal information on a large scale for the purpose of performing their duties and for work convenience. The amount of personal information they collect is usually large, and the accuracy is high. Therefore, if state agencies and their staff leak, sell or illegally provide personal information, the consequences can be very serious. In recognition of this, regulations pertaining to the confidentiality of personal information have been incorporated into a series of laws such as the "Civil Code," the "Data Security Law," the "Cybersecurity Law," the "Consumer Rights and Interests Protection Law," and the "Decision of the Standing Committee of the National People's Congress on Strengthening Network Information Protection."

I. Confidentiality Obligations of State Agencies, Statutory Institutions Performing Administrative Functions, and Their Staff

161. Article 1039 of the "Civil Code" stipulates the confidentiality obligations of state organs, statutory institutions performing administrative functions, and their staff. Article 10, paragraph 2 of the "Decision of the Standing Committee of the National People's Congress on Strengthening Network Information Protection" stipulates: "State agencies and their staff should keep citizens' electronic personal information confidential, which they learned in the course of performing their duties. They should not leak, alter, damage, sell, or illegally provide this information to others." Article 18, paragraph 2 of the "Supervision Law" also outlines the confidentiality obligations that supervisory bodies and their staff must uphold. Importantly, it emphasizes that if there is any breach of these obligations, causing damage to the legal rights and interests of citizens, legal entities, or other organizations, then the state compensation stipulated in Article 67 of the same law should be applied. Article 25 of the "E-commerce Law" states: If the relevant competent department requires e-commerce operators to provide related e-commerce data information in accordance with laws and administrative regulations, the e-commerce operators should provide it. The relevant competent department should take necessary measures to protect the security of the data information provided by the e-commerce operators and strictly keep confidential the personal information, privacy, and trade secrets contained therein. They must not leak, sell, or illegally provide this information to others. Article 9 of the "Personal Information Protection Law" stipulates that personal information processors should be responsible for their personal information processing activities and take necessary measures to ensure the safety of the personal information they process.

162. For entities such as state agencies, statutory institutions, and their staff, their responsibilities can be enumerated as follows: (i) In instances where state agencies and their staff infringe upon personal information while carrying out their responsibilities, it's crucial to recognize that these actions by state organs represent an exercise of state public power, thereby transcending a legal relationship between equal entities. Consequently, any violation of personal information privacy is attributable to the performance of duties by these state agencies and their employees and should accordingly be addressed through state compensation. (ii) If a state agency, acting as a civil subject engaging in civil activities, infringes upon personal information, it should be considered a civil tort, and the entity should assume civil compensation liability. (iii) If the actions of state agencies and their employees, which result in personal information infringement, do not align with the scope set out by the "State Compensation Law," or if such actions neither constitute the exercise of official power nor convey the appearance of exercising official power, then it's appropriate to independently apply the provisions of the tort liability code to assess the civil liability of the state agencies and their staff. (iv) The inaction of a state agency may converge with the actions of a third party and result in a joint violation of personal information—for instance, an unauthorized intrusion into the personal information storage system of a state agency takes place while the agency doesn't promptly execute its responsibility of securing personal information. In this case, the conjunction of state compensation liability and civil tort liability should be considered.

II. Confidentiality Obligations of Other Entities

163. Besides the confidentiality requirements for entities involved in public authority execution, China also provides stipulations for circumstances where individuals and entities outside of public authority may encounter individuals' personal information. Specifically, Article 1226 of the "Civil Code" stipulates that medical institutions and their medical personnel should keep patients' privacy and personal information confidential. Those who disclose patients' privacy and personal information, or publish their medical records without the patient's consent, should bear the liability for infringement. Article 1038 of the "Civil Code" mandates that information processors must neither disclose nor alter the personal information they accumulate and hold. They should not distribute this information illegally to others without the consent of the individual, except for instances where the information is processed in a way that prevents the identification of a specific individual and can't be restored. Information processors are required to implement technical and other necessary measures to protect the personal information they collect and store and to prevent the potential leakage, alteration, or loss of information. In the event of actual or possible leakage, alteration, or loss of personal information, they must promptly undertake remedial actions, notify the individual as per regulatory guidelines, and report to the appropriate supervising bodies. Article 22 of the "Cybersecurity Law" dictates that if a network product or service is designed to collect user information, its provider is obligated to explicitly inform the user and secure their consent. If personal information of the user is involved, the provider must also adhere to this law, along with other relevant laws and administrative regulations concerning the protection of personal information. Article 40 stipulates that network operators should strictly keep confidential the user information they collect and establish a sound user information protection system. Article 45 stipulates that departments and their staff who are legally responsible for cybersecurity supervision and management must strictly keep confidential the personal information, privacy, and trade secrets they come to know in the course of their duties and shall not disclose, sell or illegally provide them to others.

§2. Public Interest Litigation System for Personal Information

164. As we enter an information-based society, the protection of citizens' personal information encounters unparalleled challenges. On the one hand, the emergence and widespread use of artificial intelligence and algorithm technologies have rendered infringements on personal information more elusive, making it increasingly difficult for individuals to discern when their rights have been infringed upon. On the other hand, the protection of individual rights is impeded by high litigation costs and the challenges associated with evidence collection. Confronted with widespread infringements of personal information, traditional private interest litigation falls short in providing a comprehensive safeguard to the rights and interests associated with personal information. In response, China has initiated a public interest litigation system specifically for personal information protection. This system provides a legal framework for public interest lawsuits, targeting actions that unlawfully process personal information and infringe upon the rights and interests of a substantial number of individuals. Specifically, Article 70 of the "Personal Information Protection Law" stipulates that if an information processor violates the provisions of this law in handling personal information and infringes upon the rights and interests of many individuals, the People's Procuratorate, statutory consumer organizations, and organizations determined by the national cyberspace administration can legally file a lawsuit in the People's Court.

165. The People's Procuratorate, serving as a legal supervisory body, is vested with the right to initiate public interest lawsuits with the objective of safeguarding public welfare. The national cyberspace administration department, entrusted with the responsibility of personal information protection, has the ability to designate suitable organizations to act as litigants in public interest cases concerning infringements of personal information rights. The conditions for initiating a public interest lawsuit are that the personal information processor has violated the legal provisions in handling personal information, thereby infringing upon the rights and interests of many individuals. First, the act must constitute a civil liability for infringing personal information. Second, the act must infringe upon the rights and interests of a significant number of right holders. As for how many constitutes "a significant number," it should at least be more than ten. If ten or fewer right holders are infringed upon, protection is not offered through public interest litigation. Instead, individuals must initiate a lawsuit in their own interest to protect themselves. In terms of procedure, the public interest litigation for personal information protection mainly refers to the first paragraph of Article 55 of the "Civil Procedure Law of the People's Republic of China." When initiating a public interest lawsuit to protect the personal information rights and interests of a significant number of people, it should be limited, in principle, to non-compensation liability methods. If a lawsuit is filed on behalf of many individuals claiming compensation for damages, the compensation should be distributed to each victim.[44]

§3. National Data Security System

I. The Classified and Hierarchical Protection System

166. The classified and hierarchical data protection system refers to the scientific division of data resources based on factors such as data attributes, features, quantity, quality, format, significance, and sensitivity. It includes corresponding security risk control measures that protect data security and personal privacy while simultaneously unlocking the value of data resources.

167. Article 21 of the "Data Security Law" stipulates that the state establishes a system of classified and hierarchical data protection. The classification and grading of data are determined based on the data's importance in economic and social development and the level of harm caused to national security, public interests, or the legitimate rights and interests of individuals or organizations in the event of data tampering, destruction, leakage, or illegal acquisition and use. The national data security authority coordinates relevant departments to develop catalogs of important data, enhancing the protection of such data. Data related to national security, the lifeline of the national economy, significant public livelihood, and major public interests are classified as core national data, subject to even more stringent management systems. Each region and department is required to conduct classified and hierarchical management of data relevant to their respective regions, departments, as well as associated industries and fields. This process should be in compliance with the national data classification and grading requirements.

168. Specifically, the current regulations divide data into three levels, including core data, important data, and general data. Core data pertains to information that is intrinsically tied to national security and, as such, must not be made public. For the

44. 杨立新：《个人信息处理者侵害个人信息权益的民事责任》，载《国家检察官学院学报》2021年第5期。Yang Lixin, "Civil Liability of Personal Information Handlers for Infringement of Personal Information Rights," published in the "Journal of National Procurators College," 5 (2021).

sake of protection, such data requires implementation of markers, labels, watermarks, and other forms of processing. In addition, it is subject to stringent access controls that are enforced without exception. Important data refers to information that is of significance and sensitivity to the data subjects, including large volumes of personal data. While this data can be transferred over the internet, it must be safeguarded using encryption and other security protocols to avoid any potential breaches or leaks. Furthermore, some data is public or de-identified, anonymized data, which can participate in data processing and dissemination. While the classification and grading of these data stand as a prerequisite, the standards for data classification and grading should be comprehensive and robust, governing the entire data life cycle from identification, collection, transmission, storage, processing, provision, and disclosure to eventual destruction.

169. Six principles must be adhered to for data classification and grading. The first is the principle of "legality and compliance," that is, data collection much comply with relevant laws and administrative regulations. The second is the principle of "clear classification," which is beneficial for data security protection. Related data should be processed according to their respective categories. The third principle is "multi-dimensional classification," which is conceived from a data management viewpoint. Without a proper classification structure, the effective use and management of data can become a challenging task. The fourth is the principle of "strict compliance to the highest level." This involves different levels of data being used together, containing both high-security and low-security level data. In such cases, strict measures should be applied based on the highest security level, not the lowest. The fifth principle is "dynamic adjustment." As data types and levels may vary over time or due to policy changes, it's essential to adjust the data level and its associated attributes to match these changes. The sixth principle is "autonomous refinement." While current classification and grading requirements are set from a top-down design perspective, the application of these requirements in specific industries and fields may demand more detailed classification and grading. Certain sectors may extend beyond the basic three levels to possibly five or more. This necessitates additional refinement and specificity in alignment with local and industry-specific standards.

II. The Emergency Response System

170. China has established a data security emergency system to strengthen its ability to prevent risks in cyber security and data security. According to Article 23 of the "Data Security Law," the state shall establish a data security emergency response mechanism. In the event of a data security incident, the relevant competent authorities should legally activate emergency plans, take corresponding emergency response measures, prevent the expansion of harm, eliminate safety hazards, and promptly release warning information relevant to the public. Article 29 of the same law stipulates that strengthened risk monitoring should be applied in data processing. Where data security defects, bugs, or other risks are discovered, remedial measures shall be taken immediately. Where a data security incident occurs, measures shall be taken immediately to address it, and users shall be notified and reports made to relevant competent departments in a timely manner in accordance with relevant provisions. Also, Article 53 of the "Cybersecurity Law" stipulates that the national cyberspace administration coordinates with relevant departments to establish and improve cyber security risk assessment and emergency response mechanisms, formulate cyber security incident emergency plans, and regularly organize drills. Departments responsible for the security protection of critical information infrastructure should formulate emergency plans for cyber security incidents in their respective industry or sector, and regularly organize drills. The emergency plan for cyber security incidents should rank cyber security incidents according to factors such as the degree of harm and the scope of influence after the incident, and provide corresponding emergency response measures. More specifically, per Article 56 of the "Regulations on Internet Data Security Management," the state shall establish data security emergency response mechanisms, improve cyber security incident emergency plans and cyber security information sharing platforms, incorporate data security incidents into the national cyber security incident emergency response mechanism, and strengthen data security information sharing, data security risk and threat monitoring and early warning, as well as emergency response work for data security incidents.

§4. Other Special Systems

I. International Cooperation System for Data Protection

171. The "Data Security Law" outlines the framework for cross-border data transfer and cooperation. Article 11 of the law states that the state actively promotes international exchanges and cooperation in the fields of data security governance and data development and utilization, participates in the formulation of international rules and standards related to data security, and promotes the secure and free flow of data across borders. In addition, according to Article 36 of the law, the competent authorities of the People's Republic of China shall handle requests from foreign judicial or law enforcement agencies for data provision in accordance with relevant laws and international treaties or agreements concluded or acceded to by the People's Republic of China, or based on the principle of equality and mutual benefit. Without the approval of the competent authorities of the People's Republic of China, organizations and individuals within the territory shall not provide data stored within the territory of the People's Republic of China to foreign judicial or law enforcement agencies.

II. Overseas Personal Information Protection System

172. Article 12 of the "Personal Information Protection Law" provides a clear insight into China's approach towards personal information protection on an international scale. According to this article, the Chinese state doesn't just passively observe global developments; it intends to take an active role in shaping international rules that govern personal information protection. This not only underscores China's commitment to safeguarding individual data but also highlights its intent to be a pivotal player in global discussions on the topic. By promoting international exchanges and fostering cooperation on personal information protection, China aims to bridge gaps, share best practices, and harmonize standards across countries and regions. The law further emphasizes the importance of mutual recognition. This suggests that China encourages the acceptance and acknowledgment of personal information protection rules and standards among various countries, regions, and international bodies. All of these points together underscore the country's proactive and collaborative attitude towards addressing the challenges and intricacies of personal information protection in an interconnected world.

Selected Bibliography

Balkin, Jack M. *The Fiduciary Model of Privacy.* 134 Harv. L. Rev. F. 11 (2020).

Cheng, Xiao. *Understanding and Application of the Personal Information Protection Law.* Beijing, China: China Legal System Publishing House (2021).

Ciocchetti, Corey A. *E-Commerce and Information Privacy: Privacy Policies as Personal Information Protectors.* 44 AM. Bus. L. J. 55 (2007).

Citron, Danielle K. https://www.law.virginia.edu/scholarship/publication/danielle-k-citron/1361231. W.W. Norton (2022).

Cohen, Julie E. *Examined Lives: Informational Privacy and the Subject as Object.* 52 Stan. L. Rev. 1373 (2000).

Davis, Kevin E. & Marotta-Wurgler Florencia. *Contracting for Personal Data.* 94 N. Y. U. L. Rev. 662 (2019).

Emerson, Thomas I. *Legal Foundations of the Right to Know.* 1976 Wash. U. L. Q. 1 (1976).

Elvy, Stacy-Ann. *Paying for Privacy and the Personal Data Economy.* 117 Colum. L. Rev. 1369 (2017).

Fabbrini, Federico. *Human Rights in the Digital Age: The European Court of Justice Ruling in the Data Retention Case and Its Lessons for Privacy and Surveillance in the United States.* 28 Harv. Hum. Rts. J. 65 (2015).

Fairfield, Joshua A. & Engel Christoph. *Privacy as a Public Good.* 65 Duke L. J. 385 (2015).

Haley,Thomas D. *Data Protection in Disarray.* 95 Wash. L. Rev. 1193 (2020).

Hu, Ling. *The Political and Economic Origins of Internet Law.* Shanghai, China: Shanghai University of Finance and Economics Press (2016).

Johnson, David R. & Post David. *Law and Borders: The Rise of Law in Cyberspace.* 48 Stan. L. Rev. 1367 (1996).

Kaminski, Margot E. *The Right to Explanation, Explained.* 34 Berkeley. Tech. L. J. 189 (2019).

Kaminski, Margot E. *Binary Governance: Lessons from the GDPR's Approach to Algorithmic Accountability.* 92 S. Cal. L. Rev. 1529 (2019).

Kang, Jerry et al. *Self-Surveillance Privacy.* 97 Iowa L. Rev. 809 (2012).

Long, Weiqiu (Ed.), *Interpretation of the Personal Information Protection Law of the People's Republic of China.* Beijing, China: China Legal System Publishing House (2021).

Nissenbaum, Helen. *Privacy as Contextual Integrity.* 79 Wash. L. Rev. 119 (2004).

Ohm, Paul. *Sensitive Information.* 88 S. Cal. L. Rev. 1125 (2015).

Selected Bibliography

Peng, Chengxin. *On the Dual Legal Attributes of Personal Information.* 6 Tsinghua L. J., 78 (2021).
Purtova, Nadezhda. *The Illusion of Personal Data as No One's Property.* 7 Law, Innovation and Technology 83 (2015).
Rosen, Jeffrey. *The Right to Be Forgotten.* 64 Stan. L. Rev. Online 88 (2011–2012).
Samuelson, Pamela. *Privacy as Intellectual Property.* 52 Stan. L. Rev. 1125 (2000).
Schwartz, Paul M. *Property, Privacy, and Personal Data.* 117 Harv. L. Rev. 2056 (2004).
Schwartz, Paul M. & Solove Daniel J. *Reconciling Personal Information in the United States and European Union.* 102 Calif. L. Rev. 877 (2014).
Schwartz, Paul M. & Peifer Karl-Nikolaus. *Transatlantic Data Privacy Law.* 106 Geo. L. J. 115 (2017).
Shao, Guosong. *Internet Law in China.* Cambridge, UK: Chandos Publishing (2012).
Swire, Peter & Lagos Yianni. *Why the Right to Data Portability Likely Reduces Consumer Welfare: Antitrust and Privacy Critique.* 72 MD. L. Rev. 335 (2013).
Wang, Liming. *Personality Rights Law.* Beijing, China: Renmin University of China Press (2018).
Warren, Samuel D. & Brandeis Louis D. *The Right to Privacy.* 4 Harv. L. Rev. 193 (1890-1891).
Whitman, James Q. *The Two Western Cultures of Privacy: Dignity versus Liberty.* 113 Yale L. J. 1151 (2004).
Zarsky, Tal Z. *Incompatible: The GDPR in the Age of Big Data.* 47 Seton Hall L. Rev. 995 (2017).

Index

The number here refer to paragraph numbers.

Index

Index

www.ingramcontent.com/pod-product-compliance
Lightning Source LLC
Chambersburg PA
CBHW071354230926
51846CB00002B/548
* 9 7 8 9 4 0 3 5 0 1 1 8 5 *